# James Laughlin

## SELECTED POEMS, 1935-1985

# James Laughlin

## SELECTED POEMS, 1935-1985

 CITY LIGHTS BOOKS

Some of these poems first appeared in *Stolen & Contaminated Poems*, The Turkey Press, Santa Barbara, and in the following magazines: *Agenda* (London), *Almanaco del Specchio* (Milan), *Ambit* (London), *Antigonish Review*, *Carcanet Review* (Manchester), *Conjunctions*, *Exquisite Corpse, Frank, Harbor Review, Harper's, Horizon* (London), *Iowa Review, The Nation, New Directions in Prose & Poetry, Oink!, Open Spaces, Osiris, Paideuma, Ploughshares, Poetry, Poetry Australia, Stony Brook*, and *Translation*.

"The Deconstructed Man" ("Multas per gentes") was first published by The Windhover Press, Iowa City.

René Magritte's *Les Amants* is reproduced on page 165, courtesy of the Richard S. Zeisler Collection, New York.

Library of Congress Cataloging-in-Publication Data
Laughlin, James, 1914–
    Selected poems, 1935–1985.

    I. Title.
PS3523.A8245A6   1985      811'.54       85–27992
ISBN 0–87286–179–1
ISBN 0–87286–180–5 (pbk.)

CITY LIGHTS BOOKS are edited by Lawrence Ferlinghetti & Nancy J. Peters and published at the City Lights Bookstore. 261 Columbus Avenue, San Francisco, California 94133

# CONTENTS

# FOREWORD

> I take a certain pride
> in the fact that in my verses
> it is not extremely difficult
> to tell what I'm trying to say

James Laughlin modestly refers to his poetry as "light verse," but his is light verse, not in the tradition of Ogden Nash or Dorothy Parker, but in the line that extends from Catullus (one of his masters and the source of many of his macaronics) to Pound's *Moeurs contemporains* and Williams's "This Is Just to Say." In these clean, chiselled poems ("The rule is that in a couplet any second line has to be within two typewriter spaces of the line preceding it"), Laughlin traces, with the greatest delicacy, grace, and wit, the vagaries of sexual love, the pleasures and pain of memory, the power of literary allusion in *making it new*. A poet of many voices, he moves effortlessly into idiomatic French when the emotional, and especially the erotic, occasion warrants it. As a commentator on the local scene, he dons the hat of one Hiram Handspring, a naive and crusty old fellow, who can't quite fathom the goings-on he is forced to witness.

At a time when too many poets have turned their back on the possibility of human relationships, James Laughlin is our poet of Chekhovian longing, a poet for whom love always holds a measure of delight even as does the language that embodies it.

Marjorie Perloff

# SOME NATURAL THINGS

## The Person

who writes my poems
lives in some other

sphere he sends them
to me through space

when he feels like it
they arrive complete

from beginning to end
and all I have to do

is type them out who
is that person what is

he to me I wonder about
him but will never know.

## Technical Notes

Catullus is my master and I mix
a little acid and a bit of honey
    in his bowl love

is my subject & the lack of love
which lack is what makes evil a
    poet must strike

Catullus could rub words so hard
together their friction burned a
    heat that warms

us now 2000 years away I roll the
words around my mouth & count the
    letters in each

line thus eye and ear contend in-
side the poem and draw its move-
    ment tight Milton

thought rhyme was vulgar I agree
yet sometimes if it's hidden in
    the line a rhyme

will richen tone the thing I most
despise is quote poetic unquote
    diction I prefer

to build with plain brown bricks
of common talk American talk then
    set 1 Roman stone

among them for a key I know Ca-
tullus knew a poem is like a blow
    an impact strik-

ing where you least expect this I
believe and yet with me a poem
    is finally just
    a natural thing.

## Your Love

reminds me of the sense
of humor of one of those

funny plumbers who likes
to switch the handles on

the hot and cold faucets
of hotel room wash basins.


## Well All Right

if that's how it is
then that's how it

is & I'll just have
to put you back in

that box labelled
"wonderful people."

## The Wild Anemone

I'll call it the daring
flower its softness its

pallor so little suggesting
the strength with which

it fights the wind its
petals so delicate it

seems a touch would wither
them yet they'll outlast a

three-day storm and will
outlast I think [and now

I speak to her] the tempests
that a foolish heart invents

to plague itself because
it hardly dares to love

the wild anemone
the daring flower.

# When Does the Play Begin

*A political poem*

Mother when does the
show begin when does

something happen hush
dear be quiet in just a

minute now but you
said that a long time

ago I want the curtain
to go up hush dear be

quiet it's never good
manners to talk when

the music is playing
but mother I'm tired

of the music and they
keep playing the same

piece hush darling in
just a minute now here

eat a piece of candy
no I don't want any

more candy mother I
want them to begin the

play I want to see the
lights go on and have

the people walk around
& talk & laugh & sing!

# What the Pencil Writes

Often when I go out I
put in my coat pocket

some paper and a pen-
cil in case I want to

write something down
well there they are

wherever I go and as
my coat moves the pen-

cil writes by itself
a kind of gibberish

hieroglyphic which I
often think as I un-

dress at night and take
out those papers with

nothing written on
them but strange &

meaningless marks is
the story of my life.

# What the Animals Did

For corporate chief executives, the year 1968 was
a year of changing strategies and changing
games . . . [it was the year of] the merger up-
heaval . . . and conglomerate warfare . . . it was
one in which both classical economic and decision
theories were inadequate to explain some of the
major events.

John McDonald (*Fortune, May 1969*)

They got so hungry they all
began to attack each other

and try to eat each other
and many did eat each other

even the war and the moon
were not enough for them

they got so hungry it was
not just big ones eating

small ones some very lit-
tle ones attacked big ones

& managed to swallow them
alive it was crazy really

crazy because it wasn't a
year of famine there was

plenty of food around with
the war and the moon plenty

to eat but the more they
ate the more they wanted.

## Patent Pending

I have an invention
ready for the patent

office which I know
will benefit mankind

it is a kind of ink
and little pen and

magnifying glass so
everyone can write

a saying of Gautama
on each fingernail

and read them there
the minute that his

hands begin to feel
like picking up a gun.

## The Visitor

Tell me implacable girl
whom do you think that

your everlasting silence
is starving? you refuse

to see me you won't an-
swer my letters or the

telephone but six times
in the last month you

have walked right into
my dreams filling sleep

with incalculable bright-
ness your visits are so

wonderful more gentle
more tender more gay

than ever you were be-
fore come again and a-

gain implacable girl
my love awaits you!

## The Trout

A trout let us say
a blue blonde trout

that slips through
the bars like water

from boite to boite
from man to man but

only ones she likes
and almost never for

money and I love she
says I love exagger-

ate and her mother
asked the neighbors

qu'est-ce que j'ai
fait au ciel pour

avoir une fille qui
est de l'ordure and

she came back from
the palaces of the

king's cousin out in
Siam where they ate

off gold plates and her
whim was his com-

mand came back to the
bars and the boys and

the slow swim through
the dim light yes a

trout let us call her
a small blonde trout.

## Step on His Head

Let's step on daddy's head shout
the children my dear children as
we walk in the country on a sunny

summer day my shadow bobs dark on
the road as we walk and they jump
on its head and my love of them

fills me all full of soft feelings
now I duck with my head so they'll
miss when they jump they screech

with delight and I moan oh you're
hurting you're hurting me stop and
they jump all the harder and love

fills the whole road but I see it run
on through the years and I know
how some day they must jump when

it won't be this shadow but really
my head (as I stepped on my own
father's head) it will hurt really

hurt and I wonder if then I will
have love enough will I have love
enough when it's not just a game?

## Self-control

When questioned by re-
porters regarding the in-

fluence on his life of 40
years' reading of obscene

books the venerable Mr.
Sumner agent for the So-

ciety for the Suppression of
Vice pondered a moment

and replied: "the effect
has not been beneficial."

## Song

O lovely lovely so lovely
just fresh from a night of

it lovely oh I saw you at
nine in the morning coming

home in the street with no
hat and your coat clutched

tight but not hiding your
evening dress lovely and

fresh from a night of it
lovely you stopped on the

curb for the light & your
eye caught mine lovely so

lovely and you knew that
I knew and you knew that

I wanted you too so fresh
from a night of it lovely.

## The Sinking Stone

High in the alpine
snowfields when a

stone slips from a
peak and rolls to

the glacier below
the sun will heat

it in the burning
days of spring and

it will melt itself
a hole & disappear

in the snow I like
that stone burned

hot from loving you
am sinking deep in-

to a cold vast no-
where ice land of

your loving someone
else instead of me!

## The Ship

There is an old man in the
back streets of this inland
city who is building a ship

in his yard he has it up on
a scaffold the full length
of the yard and he works on

it all by himself after work
and on weekends it will end
up weighing more tons than

the biggest truck could ever
move they will just have to
break it up after he is dead

this beautiful ship that is
sailing now on a great river
that leads to the open sea.

# Song of the GIs & the MG

*Germany,* 1947

We are the lords of the cigarette
    & the green passport
      we do the best we can

we rule the world unwillingly
    and have good intentions
      we do the best we can

we are most of us sorry that you
    are always so hungry
      we do the best we can

we are unaccustomed to governing
    and make some mistakes
      we do the best we can

we often marry your girls after we
    have seduced them
      we do the best we can

we are hurt if you resist our plans
    for your re-education
      we do the best we can

we will help you try to clean up
    the bomb mess we made
      we do the best we can

we are the lords of the cigarette
    & the green passport
      we really do mean to do
      the best we can for you.

## Old Dr God

Sure everybody laughs at
Old Dr God and his medi-

cine sometimes it kills
you sometimes it cures

you sometimes it leaves
you just like you were

Old Dr God with coffee
on his beard & the same

old jokes year after year
and that old brown bag

that never has what he
wants in it sure every-

body laughs at Old Dr God
or that is they laugh in the

daytime but when it comes
night and their belly starts

to ache oh boy do they hol-
ler and bust out in a sweat

and send out a hurry call
for good Old Dr God!

# Go West Young Man

Yessir they're all named
either Ken or Stan or Don
every one of them and

those aren't just nick-
names either no they're
really christened like

that just Ken or Stan or
Don and you shake hands
with anybody you run into

no matter who the hell
it is and say "glad to
know you Ken glad to

know you Don" and then
two minutes later (you
may not have said ten

words to the guy) you
shake hands again and
say "glad to have met

you Stan glad to" and
they haven't heard much
about Marx and the class

struggle because they
haven't had to and by
god it makes a country

that is fit to live in
and by god I'm glad to
know you Don I'm glad!

## The Swarming Bees

I remember the evening
that Uncle Willy's bees

swarmed in the neigh-
bor's yard high up in

an old box elder tree
the gravid cluster hung

swelled with so many
thousand bees it al-

most broke the branch
and Uncle Willy sent

his boy Peter up the
trunk with a garbage

pail but of course the
pail fell and the whole

big cluster came down
right on top of Uncle

Willy's head but he
stood still and never

got a sting though he
was black with bees so

for the next two weeks
he was quoting Horace

how a wolf won't bite
so virtuous a man and

after he'd coaxed and
smoked the bees into a

new hive he sat out on
the front porch with his

shoes off and drank 3
highballs down one for

the bees & one for the
dead departed soul of

President Heber Grant
& one to the health

of that dauntless war-
rior General Principles

this all happened just
when the Russians were

blasting Berlin and for
a long time that livid

cluster hung in my mind
the black & burned and

crawling deathshead of
my youth's Old Europe.

## Near Zermatt:
### The Drahtseilbahn

High over the deep
alpine valley a load
is climbing the thin

wire to the village
that clings to the
mountainside under

the cliffs & my love
rides up to you on
such a thin thread

of hope trembling in
empty space over the
chasm that seems so

bottomless drawn up-
ward drawn upward
because you are there

so distant so close
and will always be
there far above me.

## Saxo Cere

comminuit brum a rainy day
when he can't play outside

and Henry is cutting little
axes out of a piece of card-

board he bloodies them up
nicely with red crayon and

then very lovingly one after
another brings them to me

at my desk where I'm work-
ing as if they were flowers.

# The Prisoner

Last night you came into my
dreams as wild as a bird that
has flown in an open window

and flutters in terror all over
the room what was the dream
I don't know it has vanished

away in the light but I woke
with your fright like a hand
on my flesh and all day I've

been back in the time when I
watched for each sign & each
smile was a hope for my love.

# The Mountain Afterglow

Afterglow goldens the
peak its rock beak glows

like raw blood and red
red is the snowfield

beneath it inevitably my
thoughts go to Christ's

blood which our weakness
drinks and to the blood

of another useless hope-
less war then from its

blackness the heart cries
to the peak O give us a

sign make us a sign
but back to our valley

comes only the sun's
dying glow as so softly

so delicately the bright
rock and snow fade into

night and night clouds
fold dark on the stars.

# The Hairs of My Grandfather's Head

My rich old scotch
grandfather made
his money selling

lots in a cemetery
and had a pure bald
head where once in

a while a little
stiff bristle would
grow that bothered

him so much he'd
make me stand on
a stool and pull it

out with tweezers
heart, listen to me
beware this girl who

comes bearing gifts
you never even would
have dreamed of then

Grandfather's head lies
underground it shines
there like a mirror!

## Prognosis

An old man alone in a house
full of books who spits in

the sink where he piles his
lonely dishes the children

have gone to make their own
mistakes and he climbs on

the books like an endless
endless ladder grasping at

Dante clutching at Lao Tze
defying the world of things

and lost in a world of words
an old man who stares at

the page till the words are
gone and he knows that he

doesn't even understand
what makes the weather.

## Rome: In the Café

She comes at eleven every morning
to meet a man who makes her cry

they sit at a table in the back row
talking very earnestly and soon

she begins to cry he holds her
hand and reasons with her & she

tries to smile when he leaves
her then she cries again and

orders a brandy and gulps it
down then she makes her face

new and goes home yes I think
that she knows that I come just

to watch her & wait for the day
when he does not come at all.

## The Generations

The succession of the gen-
erations fills me with im-
measurable sadness at the

most unreasonable moments
I remember about him the
most irrelevant things how

he cautioned me to drink
three glasses of water if
going to bed drunk or how

he walked up and down the
room crying peccavi peccavi
in deep anguish because he

had been with the girls and
thought he had broken my
mother's heart now I watch

my little son growing up
in my own imperfect image
and realize how impossible

it is to give him much help
in life's unending chain of
puzzles pains and disasters.

## He Lives in a Box

a kind of upended cas-
ket with roller skate

wheels on its bottom
end for locomotion &

two small holes where
the eyes can look out

naturally people are
curious what does he

eat what is he hiding
in there but he won't

ever open the lid just
skates away if someone

tries to get too close
barking dogs chase him

boys throw stones he
doesn't seem to care

he's got what he wants
& all he wants in there.

## A Letter to Hitler

Last winter we were
short of firewood and

it was good and cold
so we used a lot of

old books that were
in the attic just old

novels nobody would
ever want to read but

we found they made
plenty of heat and

twice they set the
chimney afire when

a burning page went
up with the draft and

we found they would
smoulder a long time

after you thought the
fire was all out and

then suddenly burst
into flame & another

thing they made ashes
that wouldn't stay in

the grate but floated
out all over the room!

## Crystal Palace Market

Saw a girl in a food
store who looked like

you gave me the shakes
in my poor old heart

darling darling sings
the voice on the radio

darling why did we
ever drift apart big

giant food market full
of things to eat every

thing to eat that a
person could desire

but I guess that I'll go
hungry hungry hungry

darling says the radio
why did we ever part?

# It's Warm Under Your Thumb

I guess I like it there
   perish the baubles
   there are kinds &
kinds of reality there's

the crack in the golden
   bowl & the chance
   encounter in a sum-
mer beach hotel and it's

written that the craving
   of a heedless man
   [for either kind]
grows within him like a

Maluva creeper as a mon-
   key seeking fruit
   in the jungle he
runs from life to life and

I think now I will just
   stop running and
   take it warm and
easy under your thumb.

# Easter in Pittsburgh

Even on Easter Sunday
when the church was a

jungle of lilies and
ferns fat Uncle Paul

who loved his liquor
so would pound away

with both fists on the
stone pulpit shouting

sin sin sin and the
fiery fires of hell

and I cried all after-
noon the first time I

heard what they did to
Jesus it was something

the children shouldn't
know about till they

were older but the new
maid told me and both

of us cried a lot and so
mother got another one

right away and she sent
away Miss Richardson

who came all the way
from England because

she kept telling how
her fiancé Mr. Bowles-

Lyon died suddenly of
a heart attack he just

said one day at lunch
I'm afraid I'm not well

and the next thing they
knew he was sliding un-

der the table. Easter
was nice the eggs were

silly but the big lilies
were wonderful & when

Uncle Paul got so fat
from drinking that he

couldn't squeeze into
the pulpit anymore he

had to preach from the
floor there was an el-

ders' meeting and they
said they would have

the pulpit rebuilt but
Uncle Paul said no it

was the Lord's manifest
will and he would pass

his remaining years in
sacred studies. I liked

Thanksgiving better be-
cause that was the day

father took us down to
the mills but Easter I

liked next best and the
rabbits died because we

fed them beet tops and
the lamb pulled up the

grass by the roots and
was sold to Mr. Page the

butcher. I asked Uncle
Robert what were sacred

studies he said he was
not really sure but he

guessed they came in a
bottle and mother sent

me away from the table
when I wouldn't eat my

lamb chops that was
ridiculous she said it

wasn't the lamb of God
it was just Caesar An-

dromache Nibbles but I
couldn't I just wouldn't

and the year of the strike
we didn't go to church

at all on Easter because
they said it wasn't safe

down town so instead we
had prayers in the library

and then right in the mid-
dle the telephone rang it

was Mr. Shupstead at the
mill they had had to use

tear gas father made a
special prayer right a-

way for God's protection
& mercy and then he sent

us out to the farm with
mother we stayed a week

and missed school but it
rained a lot and I broke

the bathroom mirror and
had to learn a long psalm.

## It Does Me Good

to bow my body to the ground
when the emperor passes I am

one of the gardeners at the
palace but I have never seen

his face when he walks in the
garden he is preceded by boys

who ring little bells and I
bow myself down when I hear

the bells approaching though
they say that the emperor is

very kind and not easily of-
fended he might smile at me

if I look up or even speak
to me but I believe that the

emperor rules by my humility
it is my humility that rules.

# The Philosopher

Well here's a salute to
that clean old man who's

out every day fishing up
coins with a string and

a bit of gum through the
subway gratings on Broad-

way he says that he aver-
ages five dollars a week

and he says that's enough
for a man who don't drink.

## That Summer in Spain

there was a lot of quarreling
you accused me of stealing im-

ages from your poems and I nag-
ged about your drinking but all

that has dropped away and what
remains are the funny things

you would come out with crazy
thoughts from nowhere and how

that night after we joined the
ring of dancers in the square

at Tarragona you were possessed
and embodied Cyprian Aphrodite.

## Getting Paid

The little man at the
piano in the bar gets

paid to smile all the
time he is playing and

the glistening blonde
in the Dior dress gets

paid to like it when
she has to sleep with

fat & ugly and he got
paid for selling out

his partners in those
famous deals & I what

do I get who'll pay
the poet for a poem?

# All Those Tales

you told me to make me
jealous what happened

on the raft the night
you were swimming in

the dark and what you
did under a blanket on

the airplane and what
happened with 2 Swiss

boys in that hotel in
Berne & the next day

driving in their car
and what you did with

that Italian baron in
the back seat with his

chauffeur watching in
the rear-view mirror

and of course all of
these unlikely stories

which probably you made
up only made me want you

all that much the more.

## Martha Graham

Earth and water air
and fire her body

beats the ground it
flows it floats it

seems to burn she
burns herself away

until there is no
body there at all

but only the pure
elements moving as

music moves moving
from her into us.

## Upstate New York

Grandfather says that
after greatgrandmother
had given greatgrand-

father an awful calling
down for his manners or
more likely his lack of

them he would come out
to the back and smoke a
pipe with old Silas his

hired man and say "well
Silas I guess we can't
all be Jesus can we?"

## Two Ships

What happens I wonder to
those ships we hear about

that pass in the night it
seems only a few moments

between the sighting of
their lights moving in op-

posite directions and the
disappearance in darkness

do they sometimes later
pass each other again on

the sea or do they even
someday dock beside each

other in the same harbor?

## How Can You Escape

from your beautiful body
all your life it has pun-

ished you (from an Iowa
farm to Park Avenue) it

would never let them see
you but only the beauti-

ful body to buy and tor-
ment and pursue never you.

# The Cave

Leaning over me her hair
makes a cave around her

face a darkness where her
eyes are hardly seen she

tells me she is a cat she
says she hates me because

I make her show her pleas-
ure she makes a cat-hate

sound and then ever so
tenderly hands under my

head raises my mouth into
the dark cave of her love.

## A Long Night of Dreaming

and when I finally awoke
from it we seemed to be

back where we'd left off
some thirty years before

in the compartment of a
wagon-lit somewhere in

Italy loving and arguing
soft words and then hard

words over where we'd go
next to Venice to Rome or

better to split again you
back to him I back to her.

## When You Danced

for me those steps of flamenco
there was no music but you clap-

ped your hands and arched your
back & stomped with your heels

& your skirts flew and a smile
of radiant delight was on your

face and my thoughts went back
to Tarragona so many years ago

when I joined the ring of dan-
cers with Cynthia in the square

oh she is long gone I know not
where but you brought her back

to me for a moment & gave me
yourself even more beautiful.

# The Last Poem to Be Written

"When, when & whenever
death closes our eyes"

still shall I behold her
smiling such brightness

lady of brightness &
the illumined heart

soft walker in my blood
snow color sea sound

track of the ermine
delicate in the snow

line of the sea wave
delicate on the sand

lady of all brightness
donna del mio cuor.

## The Summons

He went out to their glorious war
and went down in it and his
   last belief was

her love as he breathed flame
in the waves and sank burning
   now I lie under

his picture in the dark room
in the wife's bed and partake
   of his unknown

life does he see does he stand
in the room does he feel does
   he burn again?

later I wake in the night while
she sleeps and call out to him
   wanderer come

return to this bed and embody the
love that was yours and is hers
   and is mine
   and endures.

# In Another Country

*tesoro*

she would say with that succulent
accent on the middle o as if she
were holding something as precious
as the golden testicle of a god.


*Credere!*

*OBBEDIRE! COMBATTERE!* I guess
it was the same then every-
where all over Italy in big
white letters painted up on

walls and especially on railroad
retaining walls at the
grade crossings and to make
a good record and show how

things were in ordine they
would let down the crossing
bars ten minutes before the
trains came so people were

backed up on both sides in
crowds shouting across to
each other all a big joke
and that's how we met where

we first saw each other I
was on the up side walking
back to town from swimming
& she was on the other with

her bicycle heading to the
cove wearing her tight white
sweater with nothing under
it & her grey checked skirt

& sandals era come Beatrice
al ponte quando si videro la
prima volta there by that
bridge in Florence where he

first saw her (later one day
she brought her schoolbook
of Dante so I could see the
famous painting) com' allora

al ponte only neither of us
was shy first we were look-
ing then we were smiling and
when the train had finally

passed and we met in the mid-
dle I just took hold of her bi-
cycle and walked beside her
but you have swum already I

can see your hair's all wet
why do you want to go again?
why do you think? I said ma
brutta I'm ugly sono brutta

and at the cove she changed
behind a big rock into her
suit it was white and tight
too ti piace? she asked you

like it? the water was very
clear that day and the rocks
were warm there was a German
boy came nosing around but

she wasn't nice to him and
he went away after we swam
we sat on the rocks sunning
& talking I only knew a few

words of Italian then but we
found another language that
did well enough I'd draw a
picture of the word I wanted

with my finger on her thigh
or she on mine the sky was
clear the air was soft with
just a little breeze I was

18 she was 15 and her name
was Leontina going back to
town she had me ride her on
the handlebars and put her

arms around my neck to keep
from falling off she didn't
want an icecream mamma m'as-
petta alla casa my mother's

waiting for me so I'd better
go just leave me here ma se
tu vuoi 'sta sera dopo la
passeggiata al angolo near

the newsstand quando sono
le nove yes I said yes I'll
be there alle nove after the
churchbells sound at nine.


*Giacomino!*

she called vieni qua splashing her
arms in the clear green water vieni
subito and so I followed her swim-
ming around a point of rock to the

next cove vieni qua non hai paura
and she slipped like an eel beneath
the surface down through the sunken
entrance to a hidden grotto where

the light was soft and green on fine-
grained sand é bello no? here we can
be together by ourselves nobody else
has ever been here with me it's my se-

cret place here kiss me here I found
it when I was a little girl now touch
me here é strano questa luce com' un
altro mondo so strange this light am

I all green? it's like another world
does that feel good? don't be afraid
siamo incantati we're enchanted in
another world O Giacomino Giacomino

sai tu amore come lui è bello? com' è
carino sai quanto tu mi dai piacere?
sai come lei ti vuol' bene? lie still
non andare via just lie still lie still.


*Genovese*

non sono I'm Roman it comes from
my father look at my nose it went
straight down from her forehead
like coins you see from Etruria.


60

## Tornerai?

she wept will you come back
for me I wanted to slip away
but she found out the time
of the train and was there

in the compartment wearing
her Sunday dress & the Mil-
anese scarf I had given her
tornerai amore mio will you

come back and bring me to
America crying and pressing
my hands against her breasts
my face wet with her tears

& her kisses till the train
stopped at Genova and they
made her get off because I
couldn't buy her a ticket.

## You Were Asleep

when I came to bed all
curled up like a child

under the blanket and
when I slipped in be-

side you as quietly as
I could you stirred but

didn't really wake and
stretched out a hand to

cup my face as if you were
holding a bowl or a ball.

## Your Error

said the owl was dehu-
manization it wasn't

a girl you wanted but
a love object and for

what you were willing
to give you couldn't

really expect one that
would turn you alive.

## The Kind-

hearted Americans are
adopting Vietnamese

orphans it makes them
feel better about what

happened they did not
want what happened to

happen & did not think
things like that would

happen because so many
wise men told them they

couldn't if you had e-
nough liberty & napalm

& honor & airbombs
it's really sad about

the Americans the way
they're so kindhearted.

## I Like You

better than this she
said as we were making

love in a parked car
she was a clerk in a

bookstore where I had
picked her up & taken

her to dinner and the
next day I was on my

way to the next city
& never saw her again.


## Dropkick Me Jesus

through the goalposts of
life so sang that fair

Melinda in her soft sou-
thern drawl as she pluck-

ed on her guitar and sent
her eyes across the room.

## The Kenners' Cat

on whom I sat went by the
name of Jasper and Bucky

Fuller also sat upon said
cat but isn't there more

to it than that a cat who
holds his place against a

man must surely once have
been back in another life

a man of strongest will &
mind who was he then in-

vincible Genghis Khan or
bloodsoaked Attila was he

Arjuna or the elephantine
Hannibal was he El Bert-

rans sower of discord or
was he just another cat?

## James My Namesake

who is three comes down
the stairs reciting the

names of the months but
he doesn't have them in

order he stops on each
step to say a month and

October the month when
I was born is Tober but

it's a long time since
I cared hot or cold the

months are pretty much
alike now enjoy your

different months James
enjoy them while you

may and let the stairs
be your gradus ad Par-

nassum but always go-
ing up and never down.

# I Have Heard

the misuse of the word hope-
fully spread through the lin-

guistic landscape with the
steady relentless thrust of

lava from a volcano one here
one there at first but now

everywhere even senators &
professors hopefully post

mortem meam I'll not end up
in a hell where undoubtfully

everyone will be saying it.

## Junk Mail

is a pleasure to at least
one person a dear old man

in our town who is drift-
ing off into irreality he

walks each morning to the
post office to dig the

treasure from his box he
spreads it out on the lob-

by counter and goes through
it with care and delight.

## So Much Depends

Bill on the way you saw
the way your heart saw

what your eyes saw not
just the way you saw a

wheelbarrow or the falls
or the blossoms of the

shad tree or Floss in a
rose and 100 other flow-

ers your patients & the
babies and the measure

of your lines in Brueg-
hel's painting of that

dance so many things the
rest of us would never

have seen except for you.


for *William Carlos Williams*

## Some of Us Come to Live

inside his Cantos like a pal-
ace ten times larger than Ver-

sailles so many rooms so many
corridors the phalanx of par-

ticulars and those long gal-
leries with their endless vis-

tas of a past that no one else
has seen so well or understood

so well the mirrors that re-
flect into each other making

the rhymes between ideas yes
it is the father's house of

many mansions with its place
for each of us places for all.


for *Ezra Pound*

## Some People Think

that poetry should be a-
dorned or complicated I'm

not so sure I think I'll
take the simple statement

in plain speech compress-
ed to brevity I think that

will do all I want to do.

## What Are You Smiling About

my dear wife asked me this morn-
ing at breakfast nothing I said

nothing in particular oh she
said you're back at that a-

gain imagining you're a re-
incarnation of the Buddha.

## You and Me

that's what I wish your
letter was about not the

interesting people you've
met or your writing I do

admire your poems please
always send them to me

but in your letters please
write about you and me and

about the kinds of love we
made that summer in Ville-

franche how you remember it
how you remember us when

we were together you & me.

# The Delia Sequence

"te spectem, suprema mihi cum venerit hora,
　　　et teneam moriens deficiente manu.
flebis et arsuro positum me, Delia, lecto,
　　　tristibus et lacrimis oscula mixta dabis.
flebis: non tua sunt duro praecordia ferro
　　　vincta, nec in tenero stat tibi corde silex.
illo non iuvenis poterit de funere quisquam
　　　lumina, non virgo sicca referre domum.
tu manes ne laede meos, sed parce solutis
　　　crinibus et teneris, Delia, parce genis."
　　　　　　　　　　　—*Tibullus*, I, 1, 59–68


"May my eyes fall on thee when the last hour
　　　shall have come for me,
May I hold you with my weakening hands.
You shall weep, Delia, and when I have been placed
　　　on the bed that shall soon be set on fire
You shall give me kisses and sad tears intermingled.
You shall weep, your breast is not cased in hard
　　　iron
Nor in your soft heart is there any stone.
From that funeral rite neither youth nor virgin
Shall return with his eyes dry
You shall not humiliate my ghost, by your absence,
　　　nevertheless,
Do no violence to your loosened hair nor to your
　　　soft cheek."
　　　　　　　　　　　—*Ford Madox Ford*

# The Delia Sequence

## TO KALON

For Delia pulchra et docta
one of whose secrets I have

learned that she was in an
earlier life the lady Maeut

of the castle of Montagnac
above the Vezère whom many

troubadours admired and to
her they sang fine vers &

cansos in the trobar clus.

## MY SOUL REVOLVED

in your presence it was
not like a carrousel but

like the singing spheres
that dance through the

heavens the spheres that
Holst heard when he com-

posed The Planets hold on
now let's get back down

to earth let's just say
that you made me love you.

## ACROSS THE WIDE WATER LAY JAPAN

Her kiss came to me when
the moon was full was it

the moon that sent it?
her kiss must last me

for a year so come back
moon make your appointed

rounds to help me remem-
ber the way her kiss felt

the gentleness the tender-
ness the miracle of her kiss.


## WE SIT BY THE LAKE

and though we are a
thousand miles apart

we are very close to-
gether we watch the

water and the forest
and there is no need

to say anything but
sometimes your gentle

fingers touch my hand.

## YOU ARE MY DISEASE

not a cancer but a canker
such as afflicts a plant

like the phlox I am vul-
nerable does the rust a-

rise from the earth or
come through the air I

don't know but it's into
my blood I can't tell but

I doubt it will go away.


## YOU HAVE BURNED

yourself deep into me
I know now that you

don't love me enough
but the burn scar is

there inside me and I
think it will not heal.

## IF IN THE NIGHT I WAKE

and start to think of you dis-
tant as now you are in place

and in regard for me there is
no pill or potion no apothe-

cary's charm no alchemist's
stone that I have found to

lull me back to sleep or
bring you back again to me.


## THAT CLICK

on the telephone when you
put the receiver down with-

out answering not even one
word was like the cut of

the guillotine as it falls
on the condemned man's neck.

## IT WAS ALL

a beautiful dream that
you kissed me under the

full moon and wrote me
those wonderful letters

that you sent me your
picture & the pictures

of your children that
you sent me your poems

and then suddenly si-
lence only silence now.


## YOU CAME AS A THOUGHT

when I was past such thinking
you came as a song when I had

finished singing you came when
the sun had just begun its set-

ting you were my evening star.


## I HAVE DRIFTED

off to sea from you but
you were not abandoned

Ariadne we were playing
in the sand like child-

ren we waded in the sea
a current carried me a-

way but left you on the
shore your life is yours

again I cannot will not
harm you more your eyes

were soft & sad I loved
you as I never loved be-

fore but now the ancient
sea has carried me away.

## A Failure of Communication
## in the Animal Kingdom

A fox was crossing the
meadow and the sheep

went running but the
fox has no interest

in them he is looking
for a fieldmouse or a

chipmunk we people al-
so have such problems.

# The Child

in his little bed in
the dark room clutches

the fluted columns at
the head of the bed his

fists are rigid and he
can't sleep he is think-

ing about how some day
he will not be alive

he will not be a per-
son he will not be him-

self anymore he won't
*be* it is a terror to him.

## Dans les traces d'Ezra Pound, or
## Monsieur Roquette's Pants

On the battlements of Hautefort
the eloquent Monsieur Roquette

in his elegant occitan recited
some poems of Bertrand de Born

while the camera rolled & dis-
coursed most learnedly on the

symbolism of troubadour courts
of love & because we were follow-

ing the footsteps of Old Possum
& Brer Rabbit on their 1912 walk-

ing tour our beloved director (S.
Legree) had us do dozens of walk-

ing shots (from the knees down)
this to give sense of the visual

and when night fell and we didn't
have enough and Monsieur Roquette

had to leave next day it was sug-
gested that he leave his pants &

shoes which we would put on the
assistant cameraman and do more

in the morning to which Monsieur
Roquette gave his assent but after

some further reflection decided he
could not do it because when he got

home to Béziers (where Arnaut de
Marvoil had such a bad time with

the countess and Alfonso the half-
balled) his wife would unpack his

suitcase and enquire in which of
the Perigordine pleasure houses

he had relinquished his trousers.

# The Care and Feeding of a Poet

is a noble task (whatever the
feminists may say) it insures

the caretaker a certain immor-
tality (if the poet is a good

one) and it also provides cer-
tain rewards in the here & now

such as typing manuscripts and
sending poems to magazines and

entertaining the wives of other
poets who come visiting (while

the geniuses sit in the study
drinking beer) and in certain

cases being informed that one
or more ancillary muses are re-

quired to provide inspiration.

# The Casual Kiss

is a problem in one's
relations with the new

generation it was not
thus in grampa's day

and usually one finds
to one's sorrow that

it means almost nothing
H. James from his grave

in Mt. Auburn Cemetery
views this social phenom-

enon with much alarm.

# Cordelia

why couldn't you have
thought up just a few

kind words to say to
your dear old dad and

then we wouldn't have
to take all that crap

from Goneril & Regan
but if you had I sup-

pose then we'd never
have heard things like

the serpent's tooth &
the wanton boys killing

flies & the wrens going
to it (let copulation

thrive) & the ounce of
civit for my imaginings.

## Being Much Too Tall

I like you to be rather small
I don't mean a midget but deli-

cate of construction la donna
cosi mobile she who goes in

grace at the corner of Broad-
way & 53rd St you rose up on

your toes and said you must
find higher heels to go out

with me don't bother I like
you sized exactly as you are.

## Can You Tell

from looking at them whe-
ther they will or won't I

always thought that high
cheekbones were an indi-

cation until I spent some
time in the coalfields of

Silesia better not jump to
conclusions wait for a warm

palm and a moist eye wait
for the creeping fingers.

# Herodotus Reports

That the girls of Cimmeria
rubbed olive oil on their

bodies to make them slippery
as fish for their lovers and

Rexroth did the painting of
the tunnies from two lines of

Amphylitos & in Zurich there
was beautiful crazy Birgitte

who liked to circle the Mat-
terhorn in her plane and lie

in her bathtub at the Dolder
Grand while her admirer intro-

duced forellen and the Schubert
was played on the gramophone in

the bedroom and Henry had to
drive Marcia up to the hospi-

tal in Carmel to get the snake
out and the list of these deli-

cate practices could go on but
remember that the historian and

the poet and I are notorious
for our wild confabulations.

## Into Each Life

must fall occasionally a new
incentive to persist he writes

ridiculous letters to ces dames
galantes well what's the harm

in that he searches for the
ear that comprehends the in-

tonations that he hears in
languages he tells her that

her hands when she is talking
are the white flock of birds

En Bertrans saw that day be-
yond the battlements of Haute-

fort (touch is not necessary
for the delectations of the

mind the poet saw her only
once the old book says there

at the bridge over the Arno).

## Is It Written

in heaven that our planets
should conjoin the old as-

trologer in Madras who did
my horoscope said that in

1984 something sensational
would happen did he mean

you delicious creature I
hope I pray I do beseech

you that's what he meant.

## Love Is Cumulative

When we make love you em-
body whatever was beauti-

ful in those who have gone
before (and whatever was

not beautiful has dropped
away) so that at the last

in you it has all come to-
gether the perfection of

the sacrament (for it is
a sacrament when the af-

fection is true) such as
the poets have celebrated.

# The Junk Collector

what bothers me most about
the idea of having to die

(sooner or later) is that
the collection of junk I

have made in my head will
presumably be dissipated

not that there isn't more
and better junk in other

heads & always will be but
I have become so fond of

my own head's collection.

## Is What We Eat

an indication of what we
are or of what we'd like

to be Rimbaud wanted to
eat the air and Jarry the

noise of grasshoppers hav-
ing lived in India & Jap-

an it is hard for me to
swallow any more rice Pe-

tronius relates that the
guests at Trimalchio's

dinner put their fingers
down their throats to en-

joy a second meal & Rabe-
lais made Gargantua a

ridiculous figure (some
men like to eat pussy but

that is another story) the
mouth eats and the mouth

speaks it's more than a
paradox it's a dilemma

and no doubt people on
food stamps take a more

serious view of eating.

# My Old Gray Sweater

in the back of the closet what
will you do with it the one with

buttons down the front the heavy
one I used to wear when I could

still cut firewood what will you
do with it the Salvation Army I

guess some worthy & needy man
can still get a lot of use out

of it but you know I'd really
rather not please take it out

into the woods and nail it to
that big oak Gary jokes that

he wants to re-enter the food
chain he wants to be eaten by

a bear I'd like my sweater just
to rot away in the woodlands let

the birds peck at it and build
their nests with the gray wool

please nail me to the big oak.

# The *Non*-World

is too much with me daylong and
in my dreams my mind is invaded

by persons who are irreal all the
weirdos about whom Herodotus told

such magnificent lies the succu-
lent girlfriends of Sappho and the

tormented & tormenting in Ovid
adulterous ladies in the castles of

Provence who dread the coming of
the dawn sad sacks in Villon the

pranksters of Ariosto the drunken
and infected buddies of Rochester

it's an endless list must I burn
all my books to get rid of these

interlopers I should get back to
the real world I must listen to

Jesse Jackson and help him dis-
pose of that Hollywood cowboy.

# Persephone Wears Bluejeans

now but she's the same sweet
girl it's spring again and up

from the underworld she comes
the laurel on her brow bring-

ing the seed that will re-
new the earth and draw all

flowers and plants again to
birth she melts the snow she

calms the sea now all things
grow she is the leafing tree.

# A Small Group

of venture capitalists are
now offering shares in a

new corporation to be known
as Cyanide Pills Inc we be-

lieve that with the nucle-
ar arms race there will be

a good market for our pro-
duct among those who don't

want to wait around till
all their hair falls out.

# Why

when you put your legs up
against the wall after we

had made love did I think
of Nerval's tour abolie a

very strange and dubious
connection your legs are

lithe & lovely and the
tower is presumably if

anyone ever found it a
gothic ruin the way the

mind works is a puzzle
could it be that the mu-

sic of the poem came back
to me when you made that

so graceful and spontane-
ous movement of a dancer.

## Social Note

I don't usually try to listen
in on conversations but

the other morning when I was
having breakfast at the Vil-

lege Den there were two men
in the next booth and one of

them who sounded quite annoy-
ed said you did it again what

did I do again you called me
Warren now you've called me

Warren and Justin and Henry
can't you please try to re-

member my name is Gilbert?

## The Goddess

I have seen the goddess
with my mortal eyes they

were filming down the
street and it was Meryl

Streep she was attended
by five trailers eight

trucks thirty technici-
ans and four policemen

the whole street was il-
lumined with a heavenly

blaze she walked up the
steps of the house four

times and I know that she
saw me and smiled at me

she knew that I was her
devotee she went into

the house but they said
the next scene was in-

side and I couldn't go
in will I ever see her

again my goddess but it
doesn't really matter I

saw her and she knew me.

## Alba

I tell the birds you can stop now
I no longer need you I wake to a

more lovely music she has been
speaking to me in my dreams the

birds protest that it has always
been their task to arouse me for

the day do not disturb our lives
they say very well I tell them

you may still sing at dawn but
only in her praise you must imi-

tate her voice or I'll not listen
I will be deaf to your song.

# The French

are such an orderly race
it is reported that the

grande horizontale Liane
de Pougy would offer to

her lovers only the up-
per part of her body be-

cause the lower part was
reserved for her husband.

# Here I Am

having breakfast in the kitchen
and on the window ledge are the

saltshaker the box of brown su-
gar the butter dish the jars of

marmalade & peach jam and the
bottle of Heinz's ketchup (the

things for the body) and out-
side the big picture window are

the grosbeaks pecking for the
sunflower seeds that Helen has

scattered in the grass and the
fat groundhog sticks his head

out of his hole under the wood-
shed but goes back when he sees

the birds and beyond the fence
the sheep file down into the

pasture to browse and some days
at the edge of the woods a doe

and her fawn come to stare at
our house (the creatures of na-

ture) and somewhere far above
are the Olympians & those who

dwell on Mount Sumeru & Taishan
the angels and apsaras (the be-

ings we cannot see or compre-
hend) but they are there work-

ing their will with us yes they
are with me each morning as I

sit here eating my breakfast.

## The House of Light

has been designed by the master
builder but the workmen have not

been able to build it the car-
penters & the masons have toil-

ed for many years but they can-
not find a way to make their ma-

terials adhere to enclose light
every method has been a failure

neither lumber nor stone not even
metal or glass will serve to hold

in the light it always escapes
and returns to its source can

anyone build the house of light?

## The Hitchhiker

There's a young man in the next
town who does a lot of hitching

he really isn't going anywhere
but he's out of work and bored

so on good days he hitches around
the county just to talk to people

he tells them long stories about
himself which are usually differ-

ent he's not very bright but he's
harmless so sometimes I pick him

up just to find out what's new to-
day he told me he was going down

to Hartland to beat hell out of
a friend of his who was spread-

ing talk about him & a girl down
there I told him he'd better be

careful if they put him in jail
for assault & battery he might

not be hitching again for a while.

## To Smile or Not to Smile

She is out for her daily health
walk she is nicely dressed in a

pretty sweater & her best slacks
& a purple knitted toque if only

she didn't have to wear her glasses
but without them she can't see what

people look like her life is so
lonely she imagines that a nice

looking man the right age comes
along and she smiles at him and

he smiles back and he stops and
they get talking but of course

she could never do that she wasn't
brought up that way it will just

have to happen at one of the sup-
pers at church but it never does.

## You Know How a Cat

will bring a mouse it has
caught and lay it at your

feet so each morning I
bring you the poem that

I've written when I woke
up in the night as my tri-

bute to your beauty &
a promise of my love.

## Why Won't You Ignite

from the sparks of my lan-
guage delivered to your door

in a brazier by the boy Eros
whom I have engaged for the

purpose he is a costly mes-
senger (I have to fly him

down from Olympus) but for
you nothing can be too good.

# Will We Ever Go to the Lighthouse?

We see it every day from
the shore and we talk of

sailing out on a happy ex-
pedition we will carry our

gifts to the lighthouse
keepers but the weather

is always poor or the wind
is wrong and year by year

the lighthouse appears to
become more distant from

us until we are no longer
certain it is really there.

## The Old Comedian

What part does that old man
think he is playing he is

rather funny but not very
his act is ridiculous and

even pathetic who does he
imagine he is surely he's

not the boy next door the
one the neighbors spoiled

and the teachers thought
was so promising but there

is a resemblance I'm afraid
it is the boy nextdoor now

the old man is stumbling
and losing his lines he

must either be drunk or
sick will he die right on

the stage he's a comedian
and he wants the audience

to laugh at his funeral.

# STOLEN POEMS

*The sources of the thefts will be found in notes at the back of the book.*

## Why Shouldn't I

steal poems is the license
granted composers denied

to versifiers didn't Brahms
play around with Haydn and

this morning listening to
the radio at breakfast I

heard Ysaye ravishing the
Dies Irae theme of Berlioz

for a little violin sonata.

## I Love the Way

your curls fall down on your
forehead when you are making

love I think you are a Greek
girl perhaps you are Melissa of

Kalymnos and you are saying to
me nun d'ote moi gumne gluker-

ois meleessi peplesai we are
together naked your thigh a-

gainst mine your curls are
so soft on your forehead yes

you are Melissa of Kalymnos.

## Among the Roses

Stat rosa pristina nomine
nomina nuda tenemus & Ger-

trude said a rose was a
rose was a rose and for

Bill Williams the rose was
the symbol of Floss "un-

less the scent of a rose
startle us anew" and when

I was young if you wanted
to bed down a chorus girl

you'd send up one red rose
& a $50 bill with the man

at the stage door but all
this is really irrelevant

what the Latin says is the
rose lives from its name

and we know nothing but
names yes those erudite

barbarians would like to
take away from us every-

thing beautiful in liter-
ature and leave us only

their science of signs
arid empty dry as dust.

## Antiphilus

seemed to be making fun of
everything nothing was sa-

cred he was called a cynic
but I assure you that un-

derneath the flimflam beat
a heart of gold it was only

the pain of life he saw a-
round him that made him car-

ry on the way he did Anti-
philus was debonair but he

wrote bitter verses now he
lies here under this mound

chambered forever in earth.

## And Will That Magic World

die when you go a world
you brought me that I'd

never known before don't
go away y ha de morir

contigo el mundo mago?

## Cultural Note

O bella mia patria in Verona
there is a special box in the

post office to receive letters
addressed to Romeo & to Juliet

they come from all over the
world especially Japan and

are written in many languages
and some enclose little gifts

or photographs the writers of
these letters have many prob-

lems of the heart and there
are two polylingual and com-

passionate spinsters who pre-
pare individualized replies

hand written in Renaissance
script (no doubt they are on

the payroll of the Ufficio
del Turismo) Dear Romeo Dear

Juliet I need your counsel
and your consolation there

is this girl who does not
realize how lovable I am.

Ἐνθάδε τὴν ἱερὴν κεφαλὴν κατὰ γαῖα καλύπτει,
ἀνδρῶν ἡρώων κοσμήτορα, θεῖον Ὅμηρον

And Ole Ez said that the
thought of what America

would be like if the clas-
sics had a wide circulation

troubled his sleep and Pro-
fessor F the eminent classi-

cist had a happy day when
he was crossing the cam-

pus & two very comely coeds
passed him on the walk and

he heard one say to the other
you know what I told him I

said you remember the part
where that Greek guy was

dragging Hector around the
walls of Troy and rubbing

him in the dust I told him
I hoped somebody would do

the very same thing to him.

# Felix

qui potuit cordis cognoscere
causas I've never understood

and I guess I never will in
my teens I observed them in

terror in my twenties I was
a remorseless hunter (once I

made out in 3 different states
in the same day) in my thirties

most dutifully I begat children
and now in old age so humbly I

implore affection sending ver-
ses instead of flowers I have

never understood I never will
but the longing is perdurable.


*for H.C.*

## Saeta

I care nothing for the
resplendent Virgins on

their floats as they
weave in the Serpente

I care nothing for those
penitentes dragging their

chains I care nothing for
the military music it is

the chant of my doulours
that I would sing to you.

## Having Failed

with every other stratagem
should I now try jealousy

taunting you in these ver-
ses that you have been sup-

planted it would be useless
every messenger from Boetia

to Samos would report that
my bed is still empty that

the lamp burns for me alone.

## The End of It All

My friend the ecologist tells
me that a thin film of oil now

covers most of the oceans pol-
luting the plankton on whose

photosynthesis much of our oxy-
gen depends non sic in Arcadia

but that was a long time ago
carpe diem I say and he says

casi demasiado tarde it's too
late there's nothing we can do.

## I Am Aware

that I am a bit odd but
I crave your indulgence

and your love Cratecus
walked backwards from

Marathon to Athens in
honor of the heroes &

Peristera the little dove
dyed half her hair purple

when Eusthenes the soph-
ist had spurned her Pro-

talidas of Lycastus built
his tumulus when he was

still in excellent health
I write odes in false me-

ters using words that do
not exist but neverthe-

less I beg your indulgence
and beg to have your love.

# I Hate Love

says Alcaeus echthairo ton
erota and Rufinus boasts

that he has armed himself
against love with wisdom

hoplismai pros erota peri
sternaoisi logismon and

Meleager weeps his woes
to the night and his bed-

lamp hiere kai luchne and
these are wise words from

men of experience but alas
I am caught in that trap

for Heraclea has put her
little feet on my neck

and I cannot heed them.

## In hac spe vivo

My head can lend no succour
to my heart because her face

is beyond all wonder she is
like diamond to glass when

her eyelids part their frin-
ges of bright gold and when

to the lute she sings she
makes the nightbird mute

gods why do you make us love
your goodly gifts and snatch

them right away I marvel how
the fish do live in the sea

but patience gazes on the
graves of kings (and mine).

J'ayme donc je suis
   je souffre mais je vis

et nous lisons dans les livres
des anciens que la vie est plu-

tôt pénible pour la plupart des
gens assurément les olympiens

le savent mais ils ne font pas
grand'chose pour améliorer le

destin humain ils sont là-haut
s'amusant avec leur jeux

idiots et ils semblent se ficher
de nous mais quelquefois un

mortel leur donne à penser je
ne suis pas Hercule ni Promé-

thée mais j'ai la patience d'une
bête des champs je souffre mais

je survivrai il viendra un jour
où je cracherai dans la gueule

de ces fainéants car sans les
poètes ils n'existeraient pas.

## Love Is a School

where lovers go to learn
each other I have brought

my teacher an apple and
I want to be in her class

I'll work hard I'll learn
to spell and do sums I'll

not throw spitballs or
make any other trouble

but of course what I'd
like best would be to be

the only pupil in her
class nobody but me.

# Berenice

cried when she could not
fit her breast into Titus's

wineglass she wanted
so much to have him

think of her as a Grecian
wood-nymph but her brother

Agrippa tried to console
her with the thought that

we cannot always make our
bodies do what they ought.

## To Be Sure

there are other fish in
the sea but why are the

loveliest fish so often
virtuous o poluphlois-

boios thalasses release
I beseech you strong po-

tions of passionate love
into your winedark waves.

## Occidit brevis lux

Is it the end of the world to
indulge an old man who adores

you for you are young & lovely
and have the excitement of a

dozen who knows perhaps even a
score of lovers before you but

for him the stars are waning and
he feels the sadness even the ter-

ror of the long night that is com-
ing on he knows that nox est una

perpetua dormienda that longest
night when he'll see you no more.

## No My Dear

I'll not wish you the death
you deserve sunt apud infer-

nos tot milia formasorum
there are enough women in

hell quite enough beauti-
ful women but it is not

sufficient my dear to be
as beautiful as you are

despicit et magnos recte
puella deos and of all

these young women not one
has enquired the cause of

the world so go your way
my dear and I'll go mine.

## Nothing That's Lovely
### Can My Love Escape

How many cowgirls did the
blue God Krishna love doz-

ens the old books say and
so it is with me nothing

that's lovely can my love
escape like Baby Krishna

for his butter ball I'm
greedy greedy greedy! I

was not born like Krishna
on a lotus leaf but yet I

want to play as he did in
his palm grove long ago.

## El camino de amor

Ni las noches de amor que no
tuvimos ni tus sollazos jun-

to a la ventana there can be
love and not enough love but

love is the stronger no es
lo mismo estar solo que es-

tar sin ti without you there
is nothing yet something re-

mains caminante no hay cami-
no se hace camino al andar

there was a road and there is
a road to be found and taken.

## Ravings of the Depraved Monk
### Benno of St. Gall Who Went Mad
### from Carnal Longing in His Cell
### and Forgot How to Write Good Latin

De penetratione aperturae vulvularis
in saecula multa verba scripta sunt
et apud Martialem Catullumque legi-
mus triomphos et repulsas mentularum
superbum sed omnis corporis herba est
cognoscimus tristitiam post coitum.

*Editor's Note:* This manuscript fragment was found
recently in an abandoned closet in the scriptorium
of the monastery at St. Gall in Switzerland. It has
been attributed to Benno, a monk of the four-
teenth century. It seems obvious that Benno was
visited by a succubus, one of those demons who
assume female form to have intercourse with men
in their sleep.

## Timor amoris conturbat me

What is this vengeful thing
called Love which doth my

peace destroy puella nam mei
quae meo sinu fugit amata tan-

tum quantum amabitur nulla
they tell of Eros and his

bow but he is but a boy nunc
iam illa non volt tu quoque

inpotens noli nec quae fugit
sectare nec miser vive sed

obstinata mente perfer ob-
dura or is it not a god but

she who poisoneth my joy?

## To Πατήρ

On learning that he was about
to become a father the actor

Polycrates gave thanks to the
gods in these terms: it is true

that I never had the good for-
tune to lie in the bower of the

beautiful Anthea but she de-
clares that after hearing me

play Philoctetes in the thea-
ter at Epidaurus she conceived

the child who will be the best
singer since Orpheus himself.

# Two Letters on Samos

POSIDIPPUS TO PHILAENIS

Procne your charming servant has
brought me your letter and I get

the message I wrote to you as to
one alone as to the one alone I

could love but your answer is to
Menecratis my wife as well as to

me I understand yes as I feared
you are really in love with Polu-

cron may you have much joy of him
he is a charming young man but

when he goes please send me word
I shall be waiting here for you.

## PHILAENIS TO POSIDIPPUS

Are you Pan's goat or the owl of
Athene I didn't love my father

and it would be hard for me to
love you old man you are very

clever you talk well and your
conversation passes a dull eve-

ning but are you not cold in-
side I know all about young men

like Polucron he is only the most
recent in a very long procession

\*　\*　\*　\*　\*

Procne give me back that letter
don't take it who knows I may

need him later on that old goat
yet perhaps he *is* a wise old owl.

143

## She Seemed to Know

that she'd been designed for
the sport of Gods not like

sad Tess in Wessex more like
the rapes of Zeus like Leda

or Europa so she goes in a
gleam of Cos in a slither

of dyed stuff waiting for it
to happen and wanting it to

happen to her in a gleam of
Cos ever looking skyward for

the appearance of the God.

# Two Fragments from Pausanias

## I AM NOT PITTHEUS

nor was meant to be let
it only be written on

my stone that sometimes
I hit the right keys


## AT METHANA

we ran around the vineyard
each with half a white

cock still bleeding but
the south west wind had

already withered the vines

## We Met in a Dream

some forty years ago there on your
ermo colle in the hills behind Rec-

anati with its hedgerow cutting off
the view of the horizon you instruct-

ed me in morality and we talked of the
great dead of Plotinus and Copernicus

and many another then came a third
who sought to join us and we welcomed

him readily for he spoke of love and
of desire and of a man who became a

city much we conversed toegther in
dreams through many nights but in

the end we thought only of the no-
thingness of the infinite nothing-

ness parlando del naufragar in questo
mare of sweet drowning under the great

falls of the river of drowning in the
love that is beyond all earthly love.

# What Is It Makes One Girl

more lovely than all others
it is the light within omne

quod manifestatur lumen est
a fructive light that shines

within the radiance of the il-
lumined heart risplende in se

perpetuale effecto the light
descending to her from sun

moon and stars lux enim per se
in omnem partem se ipsam dif-

fundit the light of the ima-
gination the light that wakes

and shines the light of love.

## With My Third Eye

I see what's past and what's
to come I see you as a little

girl you wore your hair in
pigtails then telling the

other children what was right
and what was wrong & then I

watch you in your ashram time
wearing your saffron robe your

head now shaved telling those
other nuns what's right what's

wrong this is your karma this
your destiny prostrate your-

self a thousand times and say
the prayer om mani padme hum.

## At Eleusis

I was living underground
I was wandering in con-

fusion in dromena then
you appeared (perhaps

Persephone sent you to
me) I experienced epopte

the brilliant illumi-
nation you placed the

crown on my head and I
came above ground to a

new life of which you
are the force & center.

## You Invited Me

to your recital you were so beautiful
and sang the old French songs so beauti-

fully dieu qu'il la fait bon regarder la
gracieuse bonne et belle then we went to

a nightclub perhaps we danced perhaps we
just talked and at your doorstep I kissed

your hand in courtly fashion pour les
grands biens qui sont en elle chacun

est prest de la louer and a few days
later you sent me a note to thank me

for the evening and saying so simply
you wished we had gone to my place

instead of to the nightclub qui se
pourrait d'elle lasser tous jours

sa beauté renouvelle and we did not
meet again for many years when our

situations were altered and this is
the sort of thing an old man remem-

bers in quelle parte dove sta memoria
not with a sense of loss but with a

sense of gain all for the beauty so
perceived which cannot be reft from

him dieu qu'il la fait bon regarder
la gracieuse si bonne et si belle.


## How Shall I Find My Way

to your forfended place what stra-
tagem of love will compass me that

joy it seems the artifice of words
has failed what must I now employ?

## You Are My Future

and you came when I
feared that every-

thing was part of the
past I was resigned

to the descent which
beckons facilis des-

census senectute and
then you appeared as

fresh from the waves
as was the Primavera

and in only an hour
I knew that there

could be a second fu-
ture if you'd give it.

## Da mi basia mille

The boy Eros mistakes me
for Saint Sebastian he

has riddled me with his
arrows I am faint from

loss of blood and faint
with longing be as merci-

ful as you are beautiful
stop up my wounds with

your kisses a thousand
kisses & a thousand more.

# Three Skirmishes in the Endless Battle

## THE PSYCHOMACHIA

Is the way that you treat me
first enticing me into your moonlit garden
then repulsing me with disdain
a case for the old man in the Berggasse
or should we look for your cure to the
    saintly Prudentius
to his allegory in which Pudicitia,
    the virgin in bright armor
is attacked by Sodomita Libido
who would blind her with the smoke
    of her sulphurous torch?
I forget now how it all ends
it is so long ago that I read that book
and perhaps it is a story that will never
    have an ending.

## THE TAUROMACHIA

It was in Tarragona
where we danced in a great ring of
    townspeople in the plaza
to the music of guitars and tubas
    (an odd combination)
that we saw our first bullfight and a
    strange thing happened
I who should have loved it hated it
and you who should have hated it loved it
and that night we were not comfortable
    together.
But it's ridiculous, I know
to blame the death of a few bulls
for what finally came about between us.

154

Love and sleep are not usually thought
    to be enemies.
Post coetum venit somnus; after the
    frenzy a happy drifting
into oblivion, sometimes with the
    limbs entwined.
Illa meos somno lapsos patefecit
    ocellos
ore suo et dixit "sicine lente iaces"?
"And she then opening my eyelids fallen
    in sleep,
her lips upon them; and it was her mouth
    saying: Sluggard"!
But came then Colonna, that jealous
    black Dominican,
a sensual pedant and a killjoy,
trying to keep us from love's slumber
with the barbs of his macaronics.

## Tuesdays at 87 Rue de Rome

M. Mallarmé has put a curse on me
Tout, au monde, existe pour aboutir à un livre
The giant squids of the visible and of the
    audible
Stretch out their tentacles to entrap me
Make me into a poem, shouts every rejected
    object on the town dump
L'encrier, cristal comme une conscience, avec
    sa goutte, au fond, de ténèbres relatives à ce
    que quelque chose soit
It's ludicrous. Natural things won't let
    me alone
And it's dangerous to my health. This clamor
    is worse than Epstein's Rock Drill or the
    cacaphony of the Seven Tailors
Mercy, cher Maître, my head is splitting apart,
    my brains (if there were any) are oozing out
    my ears
Be kind, send me just the soft sound of the sea
    subsumed in the murmur of a shell
With your "inexhaustibly subtle speech" please
    demonstrate that the universe is a dream
I would prefer that insubstantiality to the
    punishment by particulars I now must suffer.

# A Lady Asks Me

a discerning friend
if I've been reading Marcabru & Bernart de
　　Ventadourn
how did she know or am I quite transparent
a most discerning lady, dompna de cortes
　　dig e-l dous ris.

Marcabru, the friend of Cercamon who taught
　　him to sing trobar
a crusty fellow, rather a sour apple, if we
　　can believe his vida
whom they called the "maldisant" because he
　　spoke ill of love and of women in his
　　sirventes
and what sort of a trip was that for a
　　troubadour
maybe he just couldn't cut the mustard and
　　they treated him badly
but the songs are beautiful and full
　　of invention
non amet neguna, ni d'autra non fo ametz
he says that he never loved anyone and never
　　by anyone was loved
I don't believe it, poets will be liars to
　　make a good poem.

*for S.H.*

And En Bernart was the son of the castle baker,
    a bright lad who learned to sing well
and he pleased the count and his young lady
but when he pleased the lady too much,
    the count sent him packing
then he pleased the Duchess of Normandy,
    and she him
but she had to marry Henry of England for
    political reasons
so the rest of his life he remembered those
    two ladies
the sorrows of love he knew but also its joys
    as his cansos tell
cen vetz mor lo jorn de dolor, e reviu de joi
    autra cen
a hundred times a day I die of my sadness, and
    then a hundred times come to life again
    with joy
mais val mos mals qu'autre bes, e pois mos
    mals aitan bosm'es, bos er los bes
    apres l'afan
even my sorrow is better than any seeming
    good, so that my sorrow seems to me a good,
    but best is the good that comes after
    my sorrow.

I have heard someone walking below me in the
   cellar and a voice talking above me in
   the attic
there are no young maids spinning now
there are no lads working in the croft
everything is parody, everything is the
   same and not the same
there were, there are, the times before
but will there be time coming after
don't say it, and it won't happen
but it could happen, anything can happen
such things have happened before
everything is parody, it has all happened
   before
the old poems echo in my head, the old poets
   converse with me
my past is an echo of their earlier pasts
is memory only a parody of what really
   happened?

Tant ai mo cor ple de joya, tot me desnatura
flor blancha vermelh'e grova, me par la frejura,
   c'ab lo ven et ab la ploya, me creis l'aventura
my heart is so full of joy that the nature of
   everything is changed
white flowers, crimson and gold, become like
   the cold, for with the wind and the rain my
   happiness keeps growing

An old book of fair language ful of hy sentence
   is alwey a goode thynge to poure.

# A Cento from Ajar's *La Vie devant soi*

Suis-je un faux jeton?
Suis-je né de travers?
Il me semble que je ne fais rien que casse
    ma gueule.
J'ai peur que je ne suis qu'une virgule dans
    le grand livre de la vie.
Je voudrais vivre comme un coq en pâte, mais
    je vis de bouche-à-oreille.
Je mens comme un aracheur de dents pour
    faire régner la bonne humeur.
Je pense que la vie n'est pas un truc pour
    tout le monde, et surtout pas pour moi.
Quand je pleure, je pleure comme un veau.
Est-ce qu'il faut lécher le cul à quelqu'un
    pour être heureux?
Souvent la vie me donne la chair de poule.
Quelquefois j'ai plein le cul de ce qui
    se passe au monde.
Est-ce que je finirai en queue de poisson?
Je paierais les yeux de la tête pour avoir
    une vie nouvelle.
Je suis un faux jeton.

## Dream Not of Other Worlds

this one we're in will have to
do for us there is no other ni-

hil in intellectu quod non prius
in sensu no ideas but in things

we must live on what we see and
touch and love with what we give

each other heav'n is too high
for us so let us try to find

our heaven in what concerns us
being together and lowly wise.

## I Want to Breathe

you in I'm not talking about
perfume or even the sweet o-

dour of your skin but of the
air itself I want to share

your air inhaling what you
exhale I'd like to be that

close two of us breathing
each other as one as that.

# As in Music/A Reprise/Across Time

PARIS, 1675

Madame de Lafayette, in her salon in the rue de Vaugirard, is telling her friend the Duc de la Rochefoucauld (they say that he helped her write the book) about how at the Queen's ball the very night before her wedding to Clèves, the Duc de Nemours *"had eyes for nobody"* except the beautiful Mademoiselle de Chartres. (And thence did much ensue.)

SAN FRANCISCO, 1945

And that year around Scott Street, where Rexroth lived, there was a vivacious girl who, for some reason I can't recall, everyone called "Slats." She was a bit schizzy and had been fired from her job and was on the city but she was a fine typist and Kenneth used her to type his manuscripts. I liked her and used to moon around her when she was typing. And one day she said: *"You have eyes for me*, don't you, Jim?" (But nothing did thence ensue.)

## Je est un autre

said Rimbaud & nothing in po-
etry has been the same since

but hadn't someone else told
us the same thing before with

either was the other's mine?

# Les Amants

In Magritte's painting *Les Amants* a man and a woman are kissing. But it can't be much fun because they have cloths over their heads so they can't see each other. I know two lovers who could not see each other correctly. They kissed a lot but what they saw was not really the other person. It was a person each one had made up. This made them unhappy but they couldn't stop doing it. They had to make each other up.

## Write on My Tomb

that all I learned in books
and from the muses I've ta-

ken with me but my rich pos-
sessions I have left behind.

# (AMERICAN) FRENCH
POEMS

# The Importance of Dictionaries

Mallarmé told Degas that poems
are made with words not with

ideas and that he found some of
his most luminous words in La-

rousse since I have never had
an idea and don't expect to

have one I follow his practice
but I use the Dictionnaire du

français argotique et populaire
because its words are so much

more colorful and stimulating.

## La Luciole

Je te vois voltigeante dans la
nuit et je te poursuis pour t'at-

traper tu es presqu'insaissable
mais à la fin je te tiens mais

quand j'ouvre la main tu n'es
pas là tu m'as échappé de nou-

veau qu'est-ce que tu chasses
c'est clair que ce n'est pas

moi je plains la vélocité de
tes alternances affectives

mais je ne sais pas si je veux
te faire changer car si tu é-

tais toujours prévisible serais
tu rasante comme les autres?

## J'ignore ou elle vague ce soir

quelqu'un l'a vue à Ectaban
et un autre à Samarkand le

monde est grand et plein de
séductions pour une belle

fille mais je lui enverrai
par pigeon voyageur ce mot

qu'il y aura toujours pour
elle un logement à l'abri

ici dans mon coeur fidèle.

## Pour bien aimer

il n'est pas indispensable de
faire le moulin à vent ou le

fauteuil à bascule comme nous
ont raconté nos confrères aux

Indes bien sûr ces exercices
sont amusants pour les jeunes

mais quand on arrive à un cer-
tain âge on reconnaît que ce

qui vaut la peine est seule-
ment l'athlétisme de l'esprit.

## Elle n'est plus noctambule

elle ne vient plus me rendre visite
dans mes rêves qui sont maintenant

cavernes solitaires et ténébreuses
où vraiment est-elle dans sa derni-

ère lettre elle m'a écrit qu'elle al-
lait vers la source du Nil pour re-

trouver Prester John que c'était lui
et pas moi le prince qu'elle atten-

dait que dois-je croire on sait bien
que Prester John n'existe pas per-

sonne dans tous les siècles n'a ja-
mais découvert son royaume d'ivoire

et d'or et moi est-ce que moi-même
j'existe quand elle est si lointaine

je n'en suis pas certain.

# Dois-je reprendre

du poil de la bête depuis
dix années je me suis lais-

sé aller au fil de l'eau
j'ai suivi le chemin de

l'incertitude et puis un
jour il m'est arrivé d'as-

sister à un miracle qui n'était
pas comme tant d'autres un mi-

rage dois-je reprendre main-
tenant du poil de la bête?

## La Gomme à effacer

On dit que c'est Dieu qui
tient la gomme à effacer

et nous lisons dans le Tes-
tament qu'il se préoccupe de

nous mais si cela est vrai
pourquoi est-ce qu'il n'ef-

face pas de ma mémoire l'i-
mage dorlotée de toi qui ne

me quitte ni jour ni nuit.

## La Fleur bleue

Je veux te voir comme une
fleur bleue qui sort de la

racine de l'innocence une
fleur que la vie mondaine

n'a jamais flétrie mais tes
charmes sont tellement va-

riés te laissant exposée
aux malins et aux salauds

qui sait qui sait je trem-
ble pour toi mais n'importe

ce qui t'arrive je garderai
mon rêve de ma fleur bleue.

## Je suis un cerf-volant saugrenu

je me laisse traîner par tous
les vents ils me prennent où

ils veulent de très haut dans
le ciel je regarde ces petites

gens là-bas ce sont des mecs
et des mouches je suis bien

content d'avoir quitté leur
domaine sauf pour une chose

que tu ne voles pas avec moi
ma compagne dans les nuages.

## Le Mordu de la moto

Je vais repiquer au truc je
m'en fous de cet hotu mino-

taure s'il est mortel il met-
tra ses pieds dans le plat

et tu en auras gros sur la
patate moi je peux attendre

les dieux sont mes copains
ils m'invitent à bouffer a-

vec eux sur l'Olympe tous
les samedis soir ils au-

ront une torgnole pour ce
gazier de minotaure ça

les amusera je ne me bile
pas ce n'est pas la fin des

haricots j'irai au radada
avant de rejoindre la terre.

## Orphée

Je te conseille Eurydice de
ne pas me suivre tu t'imagines

que je pourrais devenir ton
bonheur mais je crains de te

mener dans l'abîme méfie-toi
des poètes ils sont pour la

plupart des voleurs d'âmes
tu sais bien que je te vé-

nére mais est-ce que je te
regard trop sera cela notre

fatalité les dieux jaloux
ont mis leur marque sur les

poètes sois sage et méfies-
toi d'eux ils sont un peril.

## Les Vieillards

s'amourachent trop facile-
ment ils ne se rendent pas

compte de l'effet de leur
folie sur les jeunes per-

sonnes bien élevées ils
voient dans les champs

une belle fleur et ils se
précipitent pour l'arracher

et sans penser à la peine que
leur ferveur peut donner la

vieillesse est quelquefois
triste sauf que chaque rêve

est toujours le plus beau
le plus enivrant et fait

rappeler les jours verts.

## La Voix qui chante dans mon coeur

Je me suis amouraché d'une voix
mais ce n'est pas celle d'une

Maria Callas une voix claire mais
douce une voix liquide qui coule

comme un ruisseau figurez-vous
une voix qui est à la foi celle

d'une fillette un peu hésitante
et d'une déesse qui ordonne ma

vie mais quand elle me rend vi-
site dans mes rêves la voix que

j'entends est celle de Rhodope
la nymphe de la forêt qui sa-

vait causer avec les oiseaux
les arbres et même les fleurs.

## Elle dit que je mets des gants

que je ne lui parle pas franche-
ment des choses de la rue et des

choses terrestres dont les am-
ants s'occupent habituellement

elle est un peu fatiguée de
toutes ces histoires compli-

quées de naïades et de déesses
quoique j'écris toujours dans

mes vers qu'elle est beaucoup
plus belle que ces dames de

l'antiquité qu'est-ce qui se
passe dans ta tête elle me

demande je suis chair et sang
pas une momie viens me voir et

je pourrai t'enseigner comment
tu dois formuler tes poèmes.

# Elle a la tête qui danse

et c'est pour cela que je l'adore
si je lui raconte quelque chose

elle jette mes paroles dans l'air
comme un jongleur et me les rend

si changées si belles qu'à peine
puis-je les reconnaître et elle

prends mes idées et les fragmente
de telle façon qu'elles sont neuves

et rafraîchies grace à elle l'é-
change devient étincelant et le

fait qu'elle est tellement belle
est un supplément bien agréable.

## Deux Fantaisistes

se sont éprendues chacune
ne voyait dans l'autre que

ce qu'elle voulait voir
tous les deux se faisaient

illusion d'aimer dans l'autre
une création imaginaire mais

un jour hélas elles se trou-
vaient devant le miroir de

la réalité et elles se re-
connaissaient l'une l'autre

comme elles étaient pour vrai.

## L'Hermine

Je connais une gonzesse qui
s amuse avec la gabegie elle

a de la tête et s'en sert bien
pas question de fric et rien

d'escroquerie non c'est le dé-
rangement de la vie des autres

qui est sa distraction et même ses
amis ne sont pas exempts donnes-

la un menage qui marche bien et
elle trouvera le moyen de façon

ou d'autre de s'y insérer gars
ou fille ça lui est égal elle a

la bouche pleine pour tout un
an peut-être et elle est rasée

jusqu'à la gorge et le jeu
se renouvelle elle a du fiel

oui elle a du cul pour vrai.

LONG-LINE POEMS

# The Bible Lady

from Jehovah's Witnesses stopped by the house
   the other morning
she said these were bad times and that she wanted
   to share the Scriptures with me
these are indeed bad times and getting worse
   so I asked her in
I offered her a cup of coffee but she doesn't
   drink coffee
she started to read from the new JW version of
   the Bible but it's awful, all the beautiful
   words are gone
I hunted around and found the old Bible I had won
   for perfect attendance at Sunday School
   in Pittsburgh
we read passages from each one and discussed
   the meanings
she said that I read beautifully and asked
   if I had ever felt called
we read quite a bit from Revelations because that
   explains about the atom bomb and Satan
I am very worried about the atom bomb but
   she is not
The Bible proves that the righteous have nothing
   to fear from the atom bomb
the righteous will be carried up and only the
   wicked will burn
I asked her if it was the mushroom cloud which
   would carry the righteous up
but we couldn't find anything about that, they
   didn't know about the mushroom cloud
   way back then
she said, do you believe in Satan? I said
   I certainly did, I know him personally

he lives on 61st Street in New York and one of
these days I'm going to go down there and kick
his butt
you're joking she said, yes, I said, I'm joking
but I am going to kick his butt
and I told her I had read all about Satan in school
in *Paradise Lost*
she hadn't read *Paradise Lost* but she made a note
of it and said she would get it out of the library
then she threw me a real curve
she asked me if I would avow that the Bible is
absolutely true
well you can't lie to such a fine person as the
Bible lady
I said I thought that some of the stories in the
Bible maybe were myths
she didn't want to buy that until I read her the
definition of myths in the dictionary
where it says that myths are especially associated
with religious beliefs
we reached a kind of compromise on that one, that
Adam and Eve were real people, as we know
from seeing so many pictures of them in
museums
but that Joshua blowing down the walls of Jericho
with his trumpet could be a myth
for only 75¢ she let me purchase a little book that
is full of useful knowledge, such as
Why has God permitted wickedness until our day
and the reason why a little flock goes to Heaven
and the last days of this wicked system of things.

# The Deconstructed Man

Multas per gentes et multa per aequora vectus
(et multas per vias quoque aereas)
(there being no flugbuggies in the time of
    Gaius Valerius)
through many lands by shores of many peoples
a life too short sometimes
at times a life too long-seeming
the days of sun and rain and many days of
    mountain snow
the nights of endless dreaming
my periplum more geographically extended
(in Java the airplane is the god Garuda)
but I learned less not being polumetis
and my paideuma is a mishmash of contradictions
my Circes a list of fictions


Muse help me to sing
of Toodles on the wide beach at Troorak
(her hair so golden and her brain so slack)
of darling Leontina di Rapallo
taking me to her underwater cave
(J'ai rêvé dans la grotte où nage la sirène
I have lingered in the chambers of the sea)
of Dylan's crazy Daphne in the Gargoyle Club
    in Soho
(Voi che sapete che cosa è amor  . . .
Sento un affeto pien di desir
ch'ora è diletto ch'ora è martir)
of delicate moonlit Delia by the Strait of
    Juan DeFuca
of Cynthia whom I helped the gods destroy

in ogne parte dove mi trae memoria
of name-is-gone-but-not-her-smile
there in the jungle near Chichen Itza
(A ristorar le pene d'un innocente amor)
of Kyo-San (they had girl caddies on the course at
    Kamakura)
(Ma in Ispagna son già mille e tre)
a list of fictions of beautiful contradictions
Lord Krishna's lotus and Williams' asphodel
each one so wonderful so new bringing her
    particular magic
risplende ognun sa luce che non morirà mai
and Restif said there were a thousand women who
    were always one
sola et magna (mater)
Gertrude's Mother of us All
I penetrate thy temple and thou doest my soul
    restore
ineffable thou art the Virgin & the Whore
I lusted for Tom's Wendy in Kentucky there was
    guilt
his sin (if it were sin for him) but surely mine
a list of fictions of contradictions
ma basta per oggi il catalogo delle fanciulle
who cares though I cared everywhere and always
the sea was not my mother but my mother took me
    to the sea
the old Cunarder Mauretania and Bill the sailor
who showed me how to splice a rope
and Jack turned green when we were beating
    through the chop above Grenada
avoid the Indian Ocean you can die of heat

posh P & O boats are like baking ovens
the sea the sea cried Xenophon after his weary
    march
O mother sea our bodies turn to dust our hearts
    return to thee
but it's the air we breathe and now in the air we fly
what would the many-crafted Odysseus make of
    that
he never saw as I have seen from the cabin window
    of the plane
glistening Mont Blanc and holy Kanchenjunga and
    mystic Fuji
by Isfahan he never saw those traceries
of ancient water tunnels on the desert below
he did not see the million lights of cities in the night
cities now doomed to die
these things he never saw
but what he saw and did will live as long as we


I am the deconstructed man
my parts are scattered on the nursery floor
and can't be put back together again because
    the instruction book is lost
clean up your mess in the nursery my mother says
I am the deconstructed man
my older brother laughs at me all the time
he drives me into a rage and I drive the scissors
    into his knee
he has to have six stitches at the hospital and go
    on crutches but I pay for my jubilation
look mother James is doing it again he's chewing
    with his mouth open
and he hasn't learned his lines of catechism for
    Sunday

God went back to Heaven when I was twelve
   He stopped counting the hairs of my head
will he ever come back? I was waiting for Him
   then but now I'm waiting for Godot
Pound said "C'est moi dans la poubelle."
they had to chop us both up to get us into that
   trashcan in Paris
but why was there no blood? there's never any
   blood
did Abel bleed? did En Bertrans the sower of
   discord bleed
there in the bolge holding his severed head by the
   hair and swinging it like a lantern
E'l capo tronco tenea per la chiome
Pesol con mano a guisa di lanterna
E quel mirava noi, e dicea "oh me!!"
(Bos chavaliers fo e bos guerriers . . .
e bos trobaire e savis e be parlans . . .)
why don't I bleed what is it that my heart is
   pumping?
Cynthia said it was embalming fluid and she went
   away
like God and mother Cynthia went away
I am the deconstructed man
I do the best I can

Lie quiet Ezra there in your campo santo on San
   Michele
in paradisum deducant te angeli
to your city of Dioce to Wagadu to your paradiso
   terrestre
what I have reft from you I stole for love of you
belovéd my master and my friend.

## "He Did It to Please His Mother"

Tonight again I watched that arrogant man
  Coriolanus, who was too absolute, work out his
  doom
And was it nearly fifty years ago, dear Delmore
That you read me your *Coriolanus and His Mother*
And showed me how the old man in the Berggasse
  helped you figure it out, as if a man were author
  of himself
But still I'm not really sure, was it your mother too,
  for certain drops of salt, oh world of slippery
  turns
Or was there some defect of judgment, one we
  couldn't see
Which brought down the anger of the gods upon
  you, poor boy pursuing summer butterflies
Yes, you are loved now that you're lacked, now
  you've become a kind of nothing
Or is there a world elsewhere?

# Tamara

By her name she should be Russian but I think she
  is really Greek, a Hellene of the old times
for in my first dream of her she was bounding
  across a beach at the seaside
in her joy she had abandoned her maidenly garments,
  it was the euphoria of a child
she was a sea nymph, a maenad, she was Nerea, the
  daughter of Poseidon.
But my second dream of her was quite different, it
  was terrifying and I awoke in fright
in this dream she was falling past an open window
  where a man was smoking as if there were
  nothing amiss
I think she had jumped from a roof above,
  designing her own destruction
it was the same girl but not the girl of the beach,
  it was a girl pursued by the Erinnys, it was now
  the face of Cassandra or Elektra.
I do not understand my dreams, I have never under-
  stood them, they are riddles more impenetrable
  than those of the Oracle at Delphi.
I pray to the gods, though there is little evidence
  that they have any concern for humans,
that my second dream was the maleficence of a
  succubus
that Tamara is really the happy and lovely Nerea,
  sweet child of the sea.

# O Hermes Trismegistus

O Thoth O wise one
god of writing learning and wisdom
cousin of the celestial messenger who created
    the lyre from the shell of a tortoise
maker of words and language priest of the logos
alchemist of all secret knowledge
come now to the aid of thy children the poets
for we are sore beset and badly beleaguered
we cry to thee for deliverance
for help from barbarians from the three parts
    of Gaul (and from a place called Columbia)
who have infringed our borders and are
    polluting our wells
invoking thy name with false utterance
    they are poisoning our water
they beat us if we do not put spatiality into our
    lines
they put us in chains if we are not sufficiently
    asymptotic
they take thy name in vain and reprove us
    that our structures are not hermeneutic
they teach us bad words pretending that they
    are good words
O father of language come to our rescue
help us to drive out the barbarians
we need you real bad.

## Skiing Without Skis

One of my favorite dreams
And I wish it would come more often
Is that I'm skiing down the Parsenn at Davos in
  great style
One of those perfect days when my rhythm is right
  and I feel like a bird soaring
*But there are no skis on my feet!*
I'm coming down just on my boot soles
And all my turns dance to a sensual music
Down from the Weissfluhjoch in long fall-line
  swings
And no bother of unruly skis on my feet
Taking the Derby Schuss straight and through the
  deep dip at the bottom
With no skis
No falls, no mistakes, the snow is like velvet
Through the narrow schwendi in little wedels
Past the farm where the old man is always out
  splitting wood
Without any skis
Past the haybarns where the cows are waiting out
  the winter
Through the lane between two chalets where
  proverbs are painted in gold under the eaves
Sun on the distant peaks, snow flying behind me,
  always in the fall-line
Down to Kublis where there's time for a drink in
  the station restaurant before the next up-valley
  train back to Davos
No need to wash down my skis in the horse
  trough because I don't have any
Though none of the skiers I passed on my run seem
  to have noticed
The old man cutting wood didn't notice
Yes, in my beautiful dream I can ski without skis.

# A Leave-taking

My old friend has departed, he is making the
    inevitable journey
Not, I think, to dark Erebus, but to a happier
    place
Reserved for the good & the great, for our friends
    the Greek & Latin poets.
And I believe that such a land exists though I am
    uncertain of its location
Because, idiotic as they are, the gods must have
    provided it for such as he.

Memory must be my comforter, he gave so much
    to remember
As when one night long ago we sat on the roof of
    Dunster House
Watching the stars pursue their courses
And he related to me much wisdom from the
    philosophers
And no doubt I related to him frivolities about
    young female persons.
We reflected on the human condition
And reviewed the lives of our heroes, we spoke of
    the sorrows of poets
How those girls made Catullus so miserable, how
    Ezra drifted into irreality
How François got himself strung on the gallows,
    and Kleist dispatched himself and Henriette
    with two bullets.

But we did not jump off the roof of Dunster House,
    though nothing would have been easiser
Because there were things we both had to do with
    the lives the gods had entrusted to us, such as
    the fashioning of words into poems and
    sentences.
And later we did those things according to our
    powers, his great and mine small
But each of us found joy in the doing—and in the
    bond which endured between us.


*for Robert Fitzgerald*

# Tennessee

called death the sudden subway and now he has
    taken that train
but there are so many good things to remember
first the young man in sloppy pants and a torn grey
    sweater
whom I met at Lincoln Kirstein's cocktail party
he was very shy and had hidden himself in a side
    room
I too was shy but we got talking
he told me that he wrote plays and that he loved
    Hart Crane
he carried the poems of Crane in his knapsack
    wherever he hitchhiked
then his first night of glory in Chicago
when he and Laurette Taylor made a new
    American theater
I remember happy days with him in London and
    Italy and Key West
and how often friends and writers who were down
    on their luck
told me how generously he had helped them
(but you would never hear that from him)
so many fine things to remember
that I can live again in my mind
until it is my turn to join him on the sudden
    subway.

FUNNYPAPERS BY
HIRAM HANDSPRING

# Girls As Windmills

"By my count, 81% of Handspring's published poems are about women. Yet, on the available evidence, he does not appear to have been very successful in this field—far more misses than hits."

—Professor J. Roger Dane: *A Structural View of Contemporary Verse*

Yes, let's face it Handspring, my Aurelius, good
    old friend
You have been more Don Quixote than Don
    Giovanni
A ridiculous old man riding full-tilt at those girls,
    your distracted beard more menacing than your
    lance
Bellowing your bizarre verses as if they might have
    incantatory power
Laying siege to them as if they were windmills
Not of course the plump windmills of Spain
But the delicate windmills of the plateau of Lasithi
    on Crete
Hundreds of graceful little windmills spinning
    their white blades
Girls waving their white arms
Fields of young girls beckoning with their arms
Like white flowers moving in the wind, flowers
    enticing you
And in your case the boy Eros is Sancho Panza not
    Leporello.

## My Muse

My muse keeps irregular hours
Her name is Anthea which is a flower in Greece
It's obvious that she doesn't sit by her phone
    waiting for my calls
Don't call me, she says, I'll call you
And she calls at the most inconvenient hours,
    like 3 AM in the middle of the night
That seems to be a favorite time for her
Like when she might be getting home from a night
    on the town with some other poet
Naturally she doesn't tell me anything about him
    but I have my suspicions
If it turned out to be Harold Marks I would shoot
    her
But that really isn't likely because . . . well I
    won't say it . . . de mortuis in cerebro arteque
    nihil nisi bonum
She calls in the middle of the night a lot, it's
    like the old long distance operator before
    Ma Bell computerized
One ring then a little wait then three rings, I
    can always tell it's her
Anyway who else is going to call in the middle of
    the night
Unless it's Gregory Corso when he's been drinking
The last time Gregory called it was to ask me if
    I would leave him my teeth in my will

So she calls about 3 AM usually, my muse does
I have to keep a pencil and yellow pad handy to
be ready for her
And sometimes she talks so fast I can't get it all
down before she hangs up
It's inconvenient
But I'm loyal, we've been together, if you can call
it that, for a long time
I suppose there are a lot of unemployed muses
around on Helikon these days but I'm loyal, call
me Philemon but she sure isn't Baucis
After she's called and I've written down her
message I'm all keyed up and usually have to
take half a valium to get back to sleep
I wish she would keep store hours
I wish I could call her and not have to wait for
her to call me
But you know how muses are
I guess that's why old poets always had invocations
to their muses at the start of their long poems
They were apple polishing, trying to keep their
muse in line to get better service.

## At Our House

it's my job to burn the papers
this is something I've been found capable of doing
    and I do it
I'm too dumb to fix anything that get's broken or
    the electric, but I can burn the papers
there could be more exciting things to do but I do
    it fairly willingly but without much enthusiasm
if I didn't do it, it would cost a lot to have the
    trash man cart them away
why are there so many papers at our house?
there aren't just old newspapers and egg boxes and
    milk cartons and butter boxes and things like
    that
there are also many literary papers which are sent
    to me for examination by aspiring authors
and if they don't enclose stamped return envelopes
    I burn them up, I'm a mean sonofabitch, but why
    should I pay postage for their aspirations,
    almost nobody publishes the great things I write
and if they write asking what happened to them I
    say they were lost in the mail, you have to be
    tough to survive
in a way it's an interesting job burning the papers
    because I find out a lot about what's going on
    at our house that I otherwise might not
I never read other peoples' mail, it's a Federal
    offense, but you can tell a lot from the envelopes

Harold is getting letters from you can tell it's a
    girl because she writes like they teach them to in
    boarding schools, well I hope she's from a rich
    family, Harold will never make a dime
and Martha gets typewritten letters from NYC, I
    hope he doesn't want to be a writer, he'll never
    make a dime
you can see I have a lot of worries
and then I have to worry about whether I'm
    becoming a pyromaniac
do I get a kick when I put the match to all those
    papers I've piled into the burning barrel out
    behind the garage?
it's something to worry about, why I really burn
    the papers.

## The Cardiac Autoscope

is a useful and versatile instrument for lovers
designed originally for self-examination of the eye
    or larynx,
a new attachment developed by scientists at the
    Handspring Corporation
now extends its use to ventricular investigation
with the autoscope you can study your heart
    yourself right at home at one tenth the cost of
    a hospital angiogram
find out what your heart is like
no need to open the thoracic cavity with an
    expensive and perhaps risky surgical procedure
does it look like the mechanism supplied to the late
    Barney Clark in Salt Lake City
who has been proposed for angelhood in the
    Church of the Latter Day Saints?
or does it resemble the symbolic heart of St.
    Valentine's Day, perhaps in a setting of white
    paper lace with a small bird perched in its
    middle?
or even the Sacred Heart of Our Lord which we see
    in old wood engravings with the rays of sanctity
    shooting out of it like porcupine quills, an
    unlikely phenomenon in these days of doom
    and abominations?
however it looks, the autoscope will help you to
    achieve a more healthy and fully rounded
    emotional life
and at slight additional cost you can acquire the
    new Handspring multimedia model of the
    autoscope

right in your own living room, with our battery
   model or plugged into an ordinary wall socket
you can hear your heart speak as well as observe
   it, you can look and listen simultaneously, a
   unique Handspring feature
you can learn what your heart is saying as it
   expands and contracts in its diastoles and
   systoles
you can pick up and decode its messages
for the Handspring Model MM, with built-in
   minichip, is programmed to give you the name
   of the person, or persons, your heart is really
   addressing in its ceaseless succession of
   rhythmic susurrations
your heart's message may not be what you expect,
   you may be in for some surprises
can you afford *not* to know what your heart is
   trying to tell you?
can you afford to ignore its suggestions?
send at once for free illustrated brochure to
   Division R, The Handspring Corporation,
   Box 606, Norfolk, Ct., 06058
a 22-cent stamp (only 14 cents for a postcard) may
   change your whole emotional life
Handspring autoscopes are moderately priced,
   delivery is prepaid by UPS, and all assemblies
   and parts are guaranteed for one year. Snakeskin
   travel cases for your autoscope are extra.

*Special Introductory Offer*

On any prepaid order for a Model MM autoscope received before September 1, 1984, you may select as a free bonus one of the following unusual Handspring products:

"The 11-foot pole." Never be without one. Folds into sections and extends automatically at a touch. Will fit into any briefcase or large handbag.

"The Handy Home Cremation Kit." Don't wait until spring when the ground thaws to lay away loved ones who pass on during the winter months. Satisfaction guaranteed.

"The Two-toned Dandruff Dispenser." Gives you a choice for your light or dark suits. Refillable.

[ADVERTISEMENT]

# The Bubble Bed

It was my first time in a bubble bed and I was full
   of apprehension
What would it be like?
I was very uneasy in that unisex bath in Kyoto
(I liked better the hot tubs on the Big Sur with
   Henry Miller singing French songs in the next
   tub, and there were no walls and we looked out
   over the Pacific)
The word jacuzzi frightens me, it sounds like some
   bad plant-drug that William Burroughs found
   in Venezuela
Would there be waves in the bubble bed like the
   storm in the *Odyssey*?
Would I drown or be washed up on the shore of
   a strange island with seaweed in my hair, would
   there be a Nausicaä to look after me kindly?
Or what if my long toe-nails pierced the sac and I
   made a big mess in the nice lady's guestroom?
I was full of apprehension but one must meet life's
   challenges
I took a valium and entrusted my body to the
   bubble bed
Sank soon into slumber, entered the land of
   darkness, the land of the Lotophagi
Poluphloisboios thalasses, I heard the soft
   sussuration of the sea on the ancient strand
And the bubble bed brought me two lovely dreams,
   one publishable and the other not.

# I Belong

to the Best Western Culture.
As a former traveler on what was once Highway 66
(but it now has a different number)
I can attest that it is the best.
As an early lover of Lolita (in a literary way)
I can attest it is the best.
It offers a choice of queen size and king size beds
    and they are the best.
Wampum has been abolished in favor of credit
    cards
and there is a choice of two movies in your room
    each night from satellite saucers.
The German and Japanese tourists are also
    enjoying the Best Western Culture and they say
    it is the best.
But for some reason the Hopis the Navajos and the
    Zunis are not so enthusiastic
though they arrive in their pickup trucks (their
    horses being as dead as the dinosaurs) to perform
    gainful employment.
They have abandoned their blankets and their
    eagle feather overcoats for bluejeans ski parkas
    cowboy boots baseball caps and big hats like
    those worn by J.R. in Dallas.
Their new hogans are built of cinder blocks with
    tanks for cooking gas out back.
They do not seem to love our Best Western
    Culture. We sense a certain hostility, which
    troubles us and makes us sad. Best Western
    wants so much to be loved by everybody.


*for Lawrence Ferlinghetti*

# The Lament of Professor Turbojet

Why vainly do I hither fly
And yon on top of that
Like the famous chicken on the road
Who don't know where she's at?

The students seem to like my jokes
But do they really *care?*
Here today and gone tomorrow,
I vanish in the air.

They know me at Atlanta's hub
I'm a regular at O'Hare,
I sip my Coors at Stapleton,
But does anyone really care?

The coeds are a sweet delight
(Though some induce despair)
I couldn't live without them all
But do they really care?

I keep my seatbelt buckled,
I eat my plastic tray,
I'm never late to reach the gate,
But does it matter what I say?

# Highlights of the Goliad Parade

*from "My Trip to Texas"*

Two fire engines

The highschool band (blue uniforms) 22 players

The County Sheriff (in his car)

The Mayor (female) (in her car)

A car with 4 Councilmen (1 female)

The Tax Collector (female) [Neva Thigpen]

All officials have placards on their car doors
   telling who they are. Election coming. Contesting
   candidates are in cars at end of parade. Some
   politicians throw candy out of car windows.
   Children scramble for candy. Race between
   Georgia Lee Zwickheim (challenger) and Neva
   Thigpen (incumbent) for Tax Collector should
   be close.

Contingent of Girl Scouts

Contingent of Boy Scouts

Contingent of Brownies

Floats pulled by pick-ups from neighboring towns.
Decorated with colored papers and Texas Lone
Star Flags. Pretty highschool girls pose on floats,
waving to crowd. Some in bathing suits (looking
chilly) some in old-fashioned long dresses. One
bathing-suit girl has "where's the beef?"
written on her leg.

About 50 big-belly Shriners from Al Amin Temple
in Corpus Christi. Usual Shriners' tasseled fezes
and outfits. First group riding on small-wheeled
children's bicycles. Second group in small models
of antique cars. Third group in dodge-em cars.
Group of Shriners on huge motorcycles from
Shriners' Highway Rescue Patrol. Helmets in-
stead of fezes. Leader carries placard inscribed
"Drive Friendly." Another placard: "20 Years
of Service."

All vehicles dance about like bees on street while
waiting for parade to move. Several near misses
but no collisions. Shriners float. Papier-mâché
figures of crippled children on crutches or in
wheelchairs. Banner: "Crippled or Burned /
We're Concerned." (End of Shriners)

P.T.A. Float. Large schoolteacher. Small boy
dressed like the parson in *Scarlet Letter*.
Why?

Rural Electrification Float says "Job Unfinished."

Lutheran Orphanage Float. Children look well nourished and contented.

Band from nearby Air Force Base. Led by stone-faced Sgt. Major. Bound for Glory. 32 very trim bandsmen.

Rotary Club Float. (Not memorable.)

Wizard of Oz Float. "Follow The Yellow Brick Road."

The Goliad County Recreation Dept. truck. 10-ft diameter plastic children's swimming pool in shape of Texas. Blue and silver (Dallas Cowboys colors). Bottom painted with football helmet and Lone Star.

Seven antique cars, two with horns that play tunes.

Town humorist concealed in van, presumably with peephole. Loudspeaker on van roof. Humorist spots town celebrities on sidewalk and ad libs jokes about each. (No joke for visiting poet, who feels left out.) Van borrowed from Lone Star Beer.

Group of 4 clowns. "Vote for Ho-Ho / Send a Real Clown to Washington."

Group of 3 huge pyramidal lady clowns in un-designated costumes. How inflated?

Group of 3 old ladies with broken legs walking on crutches. Bandaged heads and arms. What happened to them?

Float of St. Andrews Lutheran Sunday School. Children singing "Yes, Jesus Loves Me."

Float of nearby town of Shiner. "Cleanest Little City in Texas."

Wildcat Girls Band. (But a few little boys in it.) Girls look about 12–15 years old. Very serious bunch. March and play well. Where is Wildcat?

Goliad Highway Wrecker Service. Wrecker towing demolished blue Volkswagen.

Float from Beehive with large papier-mâché bee which flaps its wings.

Small World Nursery Float. Kiddies dressed in foreign-land costumes including one Japanese, one Arab. "Children Are The Treasures of The World."

Prairie Farm Mutual Insurance Company. No décor.

God's Little Sunbeams from St. Peter's Lutheran Church. Large golden paper stars on each head.

Arena Turkey Festival Float. Live turkey tied to pedestal.

Margaret Mary Altar Society Float. Mariolatry?

Zaraoza Society Float. 3 Mex-Tex girls in bouffant dancing dresses.

Goliad Savings Bank with Money Tree. "Watch Your Money Grow!"

Pioneer Wagon pulled by mules.

An Enormous Tractor. (No caption)

La Batia Restaurant. More Mexican girls.

Float from Gonzales. "Cradle of Texas Independence."

Coleto Valley Trail Riders. Some riders snap bull whips. 6 children (both sexes) on ponies.

Cattle Feeders Organization. Mounted.

Wheel & Spur Trail Riders. Pam Hickey 1984 Trail Queen. Another beautiful Texas girl.

Goliad Police Department Squad Car. Sheriff waves goodbye to all. Cheers and boos.

(End of Parade.)

# Take Off Your Socks!!

You didn't take off your socks!
You talk about your illustrious ancestors but you
    didn't take off your socks
You have been lying about your forebears, and I no
    longer believe that Sir Malmesby d'Ormesby
    came over with William the Conqueror
I think they were only peasants, employed to beat
    the ponds all night to quiet the frogs near a
    chateau
Of course it is recorded that Napoleon kept on his
    jackboots as well as his socks but he was in a
    great hurry between battles
Even Bertrand took off his socks, cold as it was
    in Hautefort with no central heating
And there is one sock of lion-hearted Richard in
    the museum at Chalus, so he must have taken at
    least one off
Tu es atroce, tu es sans aucun raffinement
Go live in an igloo, rubbing noses with an eskimo
She probably won't mind if you keep your socks
    on.

# The Parodist

It is his thing to copy, that is his self-tormenting
obsession

He is a confused Narcissus who when he looks in
the pool sees himself as other people

He likes to copy the styles of other writers

And he likes to mimic entire other lives

If he is feeling comical he will parody S. J. Perel-
man, who could think up so many fancy words
to misuse in comical fashion

And if he is feeling amorous he will take off
Rochester or Herrick

If tragical, let it be one of the old Greeks who
could make bad or sad things mythical and so
instructive

Copying lives is far more complicated

A life is not something that sits simply on the
page, it has to be studied from many angles

What is essential in a life must be separated from
what is not

There is the temptation to be anecdotal, to parody
the most obvious gestures

There are certain gestures, certain ways of speak-
ing, which are false signs which do not really
signify

There are tracks in the sand or the snow which do
not lead anywhere

A parodist can be too personal in the choice of
his subject

He should not choose from emulation and above all
   not from desire
In life-parody it is risky to cross to the other sex
Though it can be done if there is enough empathy
   and there has been sufficient observation
Brecht's Verfremdungseffekt, the distancing, is
   sometimes a good stance for life-parody, that
   sly, suspicious man knew what he was doing
The parodist mentions no names, does not identify
   his subjects in his life-parodies, he guards his
   secrets
He knows that if he has succeeded they will be
   manifest
Can you tell who he is being today?

# Preguntas Sin Respuestas

As the Anti-Poet and his friend the poeta Esta-
doeunidienso Hiram Handspring were per-
ambulating the tree-lined streets of Talca, the
charming capital of the province of the same
name, they diverted themselves by formulating
questions—questions, of course, which re-
quired no immediate answers. Passing the
gradeschool with its designation of "Mucha-
chos" at one end and "Ninas" at the other,
the Anti-Poet remarked:

AP: Who would prefer a brothel to a school?
HH: Who would want to leave Talca for Paris?
AP: Would you prefer a dictionary that had no
words?
HH: What is the space between two thoughts?
AP: Is it true that when the horse looks back the
landscape changes?
HH: Who would prefer teargas to buying five
kisses?
AP: Would you like to have a baby in a stall of
the fruit market?
HH: Shall we dance the earthquake dance again?
AP: Would you like to turn a tunnel into a tower?
HH: Is it possible to repair a round window
with safety pins?

AP: Would you rather be the shopless barber than
    yourself?
HH: How about being a flying babysitter?
AP: Shall we join the club of the great landowners?
HH: Or would it be better to become the king of
    the bums of Talca?
AP: Who wants not to be anyone at all?

It was a most invigorating conversation, but so
much cerebration had given the poets an appetite
and they went to the restaurant in the Plaza de
Armas to put on the feedbag.

*for Nicanor Parra*

# Ein Kitzbuehler Tag (1947)

*(Some Lines Written in Ski German)*

Das Morgenrot im Januar kommt spaet
Die Bauern steigen frueh an die Kuhscheune in die
    Alpen
Kopfweh beschlagt Seine Durchlaut Edward, der
    hat zu viel getrunken gestern Abend
Heute gibt's Tanzabend in der Minerva Bar
Die schoene Bul-Bul liegt in ihrem Sonnenstuhl
    den niemals-kommenden Prinzen erwartend
Bergfuehrer Eberhart Kneisl schnitzt den Speck
    mit seinem Taschenmesser fuer seine Tour-
    gruppe am Gipfel des Jauffenberg
Der junge Amerikaner ist gesturzt and seine
    Skihosen zerrissen
Die Niederlandische Koenig'n naeht sie ihm zu
Mein Schweizer Freund mir sagt: "hoote detz het
    fiel loote oofm Berg"
Eberhart Kneisl spielt seine Mundharmonika in
    Teesalon Angelika, die Leute tanzen
Die Bauern wenden wieder in die Hoehe wasser zu
    geben den Kuhen
Das Abendrot im Januar kommt frueh
Ich fresse mein Abendessen im Gasthof Post, das
    nicht sehr koestlich ist
Die Maedl das mir serviert ist huebsch aber ein
    bisshel trauerig
"Wie gehts, Marili," frage ich Sie. "Immer
    schlecht," antwortet Sie, "jah, immer schlecht."

Bergfuehrer Kneisl tanzt mit Bul-Bul in der
　　Minerva Bar
Er erzaehlt ihr die klaegliche Geschicte, wie sein
　　Vater, auch ein bekannter Bergfuehrer,
　　gestorben ist
Es war in einer Lawine am dem Hohenstauffenkopf
Als Schnee und Eis ueber seinen Koerper kamen
Schreit er: "Herr Gott, wir sind alle verloren."
Man hat seinen Koerper erst im Fruehling im Tal
　　gefunden
Die Bul-Bul weint und muss einen Rotwie trinken
Lotti, mein Kaetchen, kratzet an meiner Tuer
Die Kirchenglocken klingen
Am Himmel sieht man keine Sterne
Jetzt schlaeft das Dorf
Die Welt ist dunkel und schwarz.

NB: Ski German, which is devoid of grammar, is
what I picked up from ski teachers and mountain
guides when I was in Austria in my youth.

# Ein Kitzbuehler Tag (1947)

In January the dawn comes late
But early in the day the peasants trudge up to their
    cowsheds in the alpine meadows
A headache is pounding HRH Prince Edward who
    drank too much last night
This evening there will be dancing in the Minerva
    Bar
Beautiful Bul-Bul lies in her deckchair waiting for
    *her* prince who never comes
Mountain guide Eberhart Kneisl cuts raw bacon
    with his pocket knife for the ski tourers in his
    party near the top of the Jauffenberg
The young American takes a fall and rips his
    skipants
The Queen of Holland sews him up*
My Swiss friend says: "There are lots of people on
    the mountain today"
Eberhart Kneisl plays his mouth organ in the
    Angelika tearoom, people dance
The peasants go back up the mountain to water
    their cows
Dusk comes early in January
I eat my dinner in the Gasthof Post which doesn't
    cost too much
The girl who waits on me is pretty but a bit sad
"How goes it, Marili," I ask her. "Always bad,"
    she answers, "yes it always gets worse."

* This actually happened.

Mountain guide Kneisl is dancing with Bul-Bul in
   the Minerva Bar
He tells her the lamentable story of how his father,
   who was also a famous mountain guide, was
   killed
It was in an avalanche on the Hohenstauffenkopf
As snow and ice rolled over him
He cried out, "Lord God, we are all lost"
They found his body in the spring down in the
   valley
Bul-bul begins to cry and has to have a glass of
   redwine
Lotti, my little kitten, scratches at my door
The churchbells ring
Not a star can be seen in the sky
Now the village is asleep
The world is dark and black.

# NOTES

The point of the notes is to show how we are part of a long poetic tradition. Old lines have echoes that can still enrich our own. The tradition exposed here is eclectic and eccentric—little wonder, since it is based so much in the Pound canon and mystique. Pound was a charismatic teacher but he never insisted that anti-Semitism and fascism be included in the package. I hope that the tradition which attracts me will also interest some others.


## SOME NATURAL THINGS

*What the Animals Did*
Plus ça change . . . : these verses about big business raids and mergers were written fifteen years ago.

*The Trout*
"Qu'est-ce que j'ai fait . . ."—"What in Heaven's name have I done to have a daughter who is such garbage?"

*The Swarming Bees*
Heber J. Grant—President of the Church of the Latter-Day Saints in the 1930s.

*Saxo Cere*
"Saxo Cere / comminuit / brum"—the famous tmesis of Ennius. The stone splits the two parts of the brain.

*The Last Poem to Be Written*
"When, when & whenever . . ."—"Quandocumquigitur nostros mors claudet ocellos." Pound's version of Propertius III, 5.

*The Kenners' Cat*
Jasper—vide Pound: Canto LIII, page 265: "In marble palace of Lou Tai doors were of jasper . . ."

*To Kalón*
"pulchra et docta"—"beautiful and learned."
"the lady Maeut"—the legends say that Maeut (Maent) was the great love of the troubadour Bertrand de Born. When she rejected him, he wrote the "Domna puois de me no-us chal," in which he described the good features of other ladies and attributed them to Maeut.

*Dans les traces d'Ezra Pound, or Monsieur Roquette's Pants*
Monsieur Roquette—working with Lawrence Pitkethly's film crew on the Pound documentary I heard the great Occitan reciter Yves Roquette declaim from the battlements of Hautefort castle, Bertrand de Born's stronghold in the Dordogne, Bertrand's "War Song" which Pound translated so brilliantly.

Old Possum—Pound's nickname for T. S. Eliot was "Old Possum," and Eliot called Pound "Brer Rabbit." A record of the walking trip which the Pounds and Eliot made through troubadour country in 1912 will be found in Philip Grover's *Ezra Pound: The London Years*.

Arnaut de Marvoil—see Pound's poem "Marvoil" in *Personae*. The pun in Pound's "Alfonso the half-bald" escaped me until Florian Eidenbenz, our Swiss soundman, pointed it out. Such indecencies could not be printed in London in 1908.

*Into Each Life*
"ces dames galantes"—the reference is to the Seigneur de Brantôme's *Vies des dames galantes (The Lives of Fair & Gallant Ladies)*. Brantôme was a sixteenth-century courtier, soldier, author, and memoirist.

*Why*
Suggested by the line in Gerard de Nerval's "El Desdichado": "Le prince d'Aquitaine à la tour abolie."

*Alba*
The *Alba* was a favorite form among the troubadour poets. "Alba" means "dawn" in Provençal, and it usually

tells of the parting of lovers at dawn, or, as Pound told me, "time for them to get back to their own beds."

## Here I Am
Mount Sumeru—symbolically, the center of the Cosmos in the mandalas of Tibetan Buddhism.

Taishan—the sacred "Great Mountain" of China. In *The Pisan Cantos* Pound gave its name to one of the Cararra mountains which he could see from the Disciplinary Training Center at Pisa.


## STOLEN POEMS

### I Love The Way
"nun d'ote moi gumne glukerois meleesi peplesai"— "and now you are close to me naked with your lovely limbs." From Rufinus, in *The Greek Anthology*, V, 47.

### Among the Roses
"State rosa pristina . . ."—essentially, "it's the name which makes the thing." From Umberto Eco's *The Name of the Rose,* and he apparently found it in a lugubrious long poem by the medieval monk Bernard of Cluny, *De contemptu mundi.*

"unless the scent of a rose" is from the end of Book V of Williams's *Paterson.* The rose is a symbol for his wife, Floss.

### And Will That Magic World
"Y ha de morir" is from Machado.

### Cultural Note
For the basis of this unlikely story see H. V. Morton: *A Traveller in Italy,* New York, 1964, pages 304–5. Morton repeats the libel that the sarcophagus in the abandoned monastery near the Portoni della Brà is really a beautified horse-trough, but *I know* that

> ". . . here lies Juliet, and her beauty makes
> This vault a feasting presence full of light."

"per cui tanto piansero i cuori gentili e i poeti cantarano."

Ἐνθάδε τὴν ἱερὴν κεφαλὴν κατὰ γαῖα καλύπτει, ἀνδρῶν ἡρώων
κοσμήτορα, θεῖον Ὅμηρον

The title is from *The Greek Anthology*, VIII, 3: "Now
the earth covers that sacred man, the divine Homer,
who marshalled the heroes."

Lines 2–4 are from Pound's "Cantico del Sole."

Professor F is Robert Fitzgerald, who told me the story.

*Felix*
"Felix qui potuit cordis cognoscere causas"—"Happy he
who can understand the reasons of the heart"—is a pun
on Virgil's tribute to Lucretius (*Georgics*, II, 490):
"Felix qui potuit rerum cognoscere causas"—"Happy
this man who understood the causes of things (in na-
ture)." The poem flows out of the pun.

*Saeta*
Feria de la Semana Santa in Seville.

*The End of It All*
The "ecologist" is the Chilean poet Nicanor Parra.

*I Hate Love*
From *The Greek Anthology*, V, 8, 10, 93

*In hac spe vivo*
All of the phrases, except the connectives, are, with
some modification, from *Pericles*.

The patchwork *cento*, a poem composed with passages
from an earlier author, has an ancient lineage. In the
*Princeton Encyclopedia*, R. J. Getty tells us that the
earliest known example is by one Trygaeus, who made
his own poem with lines from the *Iliad* and the *Odyssey*.
Virgil was much "centoed," as in the *Cento nuptialis* of
Ausonius. In Italy there was a *Petrarca spirituale* (1536)
and in England a *Cicero princeps* (1608). See J. O. Dele-
pierre, *Tableau de la littérature du centon chez les an-*

*ciens et chez les modernes* (1874–75), and R. Lamacchia, "Dell'arte allusiva al centone," *Atene e Roma,* n.s. 3 (1958).

*J'ayme donc je suis je souffre mais je vis*
"J'ayme donc je suis"—the motto which Pound had on his stationery when he was confined in St Elizabeths Hospital. Apparently not Old French but from "amo ergo sum" in Canto LXXX, and before that, of course, from Descartes: "Cogito ergo sum."

*Love Is a School*
"Love is a school . . ."—"Night Letters, IV," in Thomas Merton's *18 Poems* (1986).

*Berenice*
Racine's *Berenice,* recalled by a contemporary instance.

*To Be Sure*
"o poluphloisboios thalasses"—"the loud-roaring sea." One of Pound's favorite tags from Homer (*Iliad,* I, 34). See "Stele" (*Personae,* page 181) and in the *Cantos.*

*Occidit brevis lux*
From Catullus, V.

*No My Dear*
"sunt apud infernos. . ."—Propertius, III, 26

"despicit et magnos. . ."—Propertius, II, 32

Pound's rescriptions (the *Homage to Sextus Propertius* was *not* intended to be a translation) follow the Latin lines. The passages will be found on pages 223 and 228 of *Personae.*

*Nothing That's Lovely Can My Love Escape*
Stolen from various books about the Hindu gods. For the Krishna stories see Nivedita & Coomaraswamy, *Myths of the Hindus and Buddhists.* I brought back from India a little bronze baby Krishna playing with his butter ball and a Telagu glass painting of Krishna on his lotus

leaf guarded by a cobra. Krishna's favorite among the gopis who herded the kine was Radha. The love duets of Krishna and Radha are the basis of Bengali poetry. See *In Praise of Krishna*, translated by E. C. Dimock, Jr., & Denise Levertov.

*El camino de amor*
"Ni las noches . . ."—"Neither the nights of love that we did not have, nor your sobbing beside the window. . ." (Neruda)

"No es lo mismo. . ."—"It is not the same to be alone and to be without you." (Enrique Lihn)

"Caminante. . ."—"Traveller, there is no road, the road is made when we walk on it." (Machado)

*The Ravings of the Depraved Monk*
The Latin, such as it is, is not suitable for the family audience.

*Timor amoris conturbat me*
"Timor amoris conturbat me"—"the fear of love disquiets me." A pun on "timor mortis conturbat me," the refrain of William Dunbar's "Lament for the Makers."

"puella nam mei. . ."—Catullus, XXXVII, 11-12. "My girl who has left me, though she was loved as she will never be loved again."

"nunc iam illa. . ."—Catullus, VIII, 10–11. "Don't chase after her, or be miserable, but with your mind set be firm and endure."

To Πατήρ
*To Pater*—"the father"

*Two Letters on Samos*
The names of the characters are from *The Greek Anthology*, but the story is contemporary.

*She Seemed to Know*
"In a gleam of Cos / in a slither of dyed stuff"—Pound's

rescription of Propertius, 1,2,2: "et tenues Cosa veste movere sinus."

Drawn from Hardy, *Tess of the D'Urbervilles*, at the end: ". . . the President of the Immortals . . . had ended his sport with Tess."

*Two Fragments from Pausanias*
Pausanias—the Greek traveler and geographer of the second century A.D.

Pittheus—in Greek legend, the king of Troezen, said to be the wisest man of his time.

*We Met in A Dream*
"ermo colle . . ."—the first lines of Leopardi's "L'Infinito" are: "Sempre caro mi fu quest'ermo colle, / E questa siepe, che da tante parte / Dell'ultimo orizzonte il guardo esclude." "Always dear to me was this lonely hill / and this hedgerow which hides so much / of the distant horizon from my sight."

Leopardi's *Operette morali* were prose pieces as rich as prose-poetry in which he set forth his personal philosophy, often in dialogues with the great dead (Plotinus, Copernicus) which imitated the style of Lucian. He called them "the true harvest of my life."

"of love and of desire . . ."—see William Carlos Williams's poem "Perpetuum Mobile: The City." . . . "a man who became a city"—see the author's note to *Paterson*. Williams would have known Leopardi's "L'Infinito" through his friend Kenneth Rexroth's translation of it.

"nothingness"—see Thomas Merton and D. T. Suzuki, *Wisdom in Emptiness*; the Zen concept descends, of course, from Madhyamika *sunyata*.

"naufragar" (from the Latin *navis frangere*—to break up the ship). The last line of "L'Infinito," surely one of the finest lines in Italian poetry, is: "E il naufragar m'è dolce in questo mare." "And it is sweet for me to sink in that sea" (of infinity).

"great falls"—Williams's Great Falls of the Passaic River; the theme of "death by water" in *Paterson*.

"beyond all earthly love"—the message of Dante's *Paradiso*. The final line is: "L'Amor che move il sole e l'altre stelle"—"That Love which moves the sun and the other stars."

*What Is It Makes One Girl*
The greater part of this poem is stolen from Hugh Kenner's *The Pound Era*, pages 451-52.

"Omne quod manifestatur . . ."—*Ephesians*, V, 13. "All that is manifest is light."

"Risplende in sè . . ."—from Guido Cavalcanti's "Donna mi priegha" canzone. The lady has asked the poet to tell her "of an affect that comes often and is fell . . . Love by name." And in part of his response he tells how Love in "spreading its rays . . . is its own effect unendingly . . ." (Pound's translation).

"The light descending . . ." Pound's explication, in his Confucian "Terminology," of the Chinese character 朙

"The light descending (from the sun, moon, and stars). To be watched as component in ideogram indicating spirits, rites, ceremonies."

"Lux enim per se . . ." Bishop Robert Grosseteste (c. 1170–1253). "For light by its nature pours forth itself into every region."

The last three lines are a rescription from William Carlos Williams's "Asphodel, That Greeny Flower," *Pictures from Brueghel*, Pages 181–82.

*With My Third Eye*
Stolen from various books on Tibetan and Tantric Buddhism. "Om mani padme hum" is the best known of the Tibetan Buddhist mantras. The novice aspiring to dzogchen, the "great perfection," prostrates himself 100,000 times while chanting the mantra, which means, literally, "the jewel at the heart of the lotus," but has

many symbolic ramifications. The concept of the (mystical) Third Eye appears to have begun as magic in the Swat Valley of India and was probably brought to Tibet in the eighth century A.D. by Padma Sambhava, the "great guru," who sold it to the hardy but superstitious mountaineers. An ashram is an Indian hermitage. "Ashram time" is the fourth and last stage of the Brahmanical scheme of life, when the householder leaves his family and becomes a hermit (vanaprastha) or homeless mendicant (sannyasi).

*At Eleusis*
*dromena & epopte.* My thanks to Kay Davis for her treatment of the Eleusinian Mysteries in *Fugue and Fresco: Structures in Pound's Cantos.* Actually Pound had told me about the mysteries in 1935, though his account was confused with the theory he had appended to his translation of De Gourmont's *Physique de l'amour* about creativity coming from sperm which rose to the brain. Is this whole idea one of his leg-pulls?

*You Invited Me*
"Dieu qu'il la fait bon regarder"—from Charles D'Orléans (1391–1465).

"In quella parte dove sta memoria"—from Guido Cavalcanti (c. 1250–1300), the "Donna mi pregha" canzone.

"Cannot be reft from him"—distorted from Ezra Pound, Canto LXXXI.

*Write on My Tomb*
ταυτ .ἔκω ὅσσ᾽ εμαθον καὶ ἐφρόντισα, καὶ μετὰ Μουσῶν
σέμν᾽ ἐδάην. τὰ δὲ πολλὰ καὶ ὅλβια τῦθος ἐμαρψεν.

Very freely from Crates of Thebes, *The Greek Anthology,* VII, 326.

*You Are My Future*
"the descent beckons . . ."—from William Carlos Williams, "The Descent."

"facilis descensus . . ."—a corruption of Virgil's "facilis descensus Averno," here "the descent into senility is easy."

*Da Mi Basia Mille*
"Da mi basia mille"—from Catullus, V.

*Three Skirmishes in the Endless Battle*
Psychomachia—the conflict of the soul with the body. A conventional subject for Christian-Latin poetry of the Middle Ages.

Tauromachia—a bullfight.

Hypnerotomachia—the battle between sleep and love. One of Aldus's most beautiful editions was the *Hypnerotomachia Poliphili* (1499) "a bizarre and curious mixture of pedantry and sensualism by a Dominican monk named Francesco Colonna, who wrote in Italian weirdly mixed with Latin, Greek, and even Hebrew" (D. C. McMurtrie: *The Book*).

"post coetum venit somnus"—after love comes sleep.

"illa meos somno . . ."—Propertius, VII, 7–9. And Pound's rescription of the lines on page 220 of *Personae*.

*How Shall I Find My Way*
"forfended place"—from *King Lear*.

*Tuesdays at 87 Rue de Rome*
Stolen from Hugh Kenner, *A Colder Eye*, pages 144–45.

Schuldorff, in *Die Morphologie des Verbrechertumsgeisteshaltung*, cites the case of Steinbrenner, who stole only for the sexual satisfaction of confessing his crime to his victim. We see this also in certain films in which the mastermind criminal plots a perfect crime but leaves some clue for the detective because he *wishes* to be caught.

It is impossible to translate Mallarmé.

*A Lady Asks Me*
"A lady asks me"—the opening line of Guido Caval-
canti's "Donna mi pregha" canzone.

Marcabru—one of the twelfth-century troubadours.

"non amet neguna . . ."—from "Dirai vos senes dup-
tansa" of Marcabru, the last line.

Bernhart de Ventadourn—another twelfth-century
troubadour.

"mais val mos mals . . ."—from "Non es meravelha
s'eu chan" of Bernhart de Ventadourn, the fourth stanza.
I find it impossible to approximate the sounds of the
short, stabbing Provençal words because the English
words which take the meaning are too long.

"I have heard someone walking . . ."—parody of Eliot's
tone in *Four Quartets.*

"tant ai mo cor . . ."—from "Tant ai mo cor ple de
joya" of Bernhart de Ventadourn, the first stanza.

"An old book of fair language . . ."—parody of
Chaucer.

*A Cento from Ajar's La Vie devant soi*
Romain Gary, after becoming one of the most famous
writers in France, announced: "J'étais fatigué de la
gueule qu'on m'avait donné" ("I was tired of the mug
which [the critics] had given me") and, in the greatest
secrecy, wrote four novels under the name of Emile
Ajar. The true authorship was not recognized until
after his death, when his "Ajar confession" was pub-
lished by his son.

*Dream Not of Other Worlds*
From *Paradise Lost,* Book VIII, Raphael's advice to
Adam:

> "Heav'n is for thee too high
> To know what passes there, be lowly wise:
> Think only what concerns thee and thy being;
> Dream not of Other Worlds . . ."

"nihil in intellectu . . ." Probably from one of the Scholastics, which William Carlos Williams may have known for his "no ideas but in things."

## I Want to Breathe
The Greeks believed that the pneuma (air/breath) was a spirit superior to both body and soul, and the Stoics held that it was an ethereal fiery stuff, a cosmic principle.

## Je est un autre
"Je est un autre"—from Rimbaud's letter to his friend Izambard of May 13, 1871. Rimbaud wrote "Je est" instead of the normal "Je suis" ("I is" instead of "I am"), meaning, I think, that he wanted to be two people.

"either was the other's mine"—from "The Phoenix and The Turtle," attributed to Shakespeare.

(Of course, Rimbaud is making two out of one, while Shakespeare is making one out of two, but this is the computer age, and both of these operations are in the binary system.)

> How now, young Flavius, whence come these
> depraved fancies?

> Oh no, Sir, I mean yes, Sir, they come
> from my computer professor, Sir, from
> the learned Doctor Kenner.

> Pox on the fellow, he's a Ranter, and a
> scoundrel. He's another Socrates.

> Yes, Sir, I mean no, Sir, he's a very
> kind gentleman, Sir, and he's kind to
> cats. He has a capacious heart, Sir.

## FRENCH POEMS

## La Gomme à effacer
Gomme à effacer—an eraser.

The first two lines are from Emile Ajar's *La Vie devant soi*.

*La Fleure bleue*
*Les fleurs bleues*—roman de Raymond Queneau.


LONG–LINE POEMS

*The Deconstructed Man*
"Multas per gentes . . ."—Catullus, CI, the elegy for his brother. "By strangers' coasts and waters, many days at sea" (Robert Fitzgerald's version). The next line was composed by Fitzgerald in our golfcart in Carolina, on request for how Catullus would deal with airplane travel.

polumetis—the Homeric epithet for Odysseus, the man of many counsels.

Troorak—a beach town near Sydney, Australia.

Rapallo—a seaside town near Genova where Pound lived for many years.

"J'ai rêvé dans la grotte . . ."—Gerard de Nerval: "El Desdichado." "I was dreaming in the grotto where the mermaids swim."

"I have lingered . . ."—Eliot: "Prufrock." The lines inspired by Nerval.

"Voi che sapete . . ."—Cherubino's aria in Mozart's *The Marriage of Figaro*.

in Ogne parte . . . —"in every place where memory leads me." Suggested by the lines in Cavalcanti's "Donna mi pregha": "In quelle parte dove sta memoria."

"A ristorar le pene . . ."—Zerlina's duet in Mozart's *Don Giovanni*.

"Ma in Ispagna . . ."—Leporello's patter song in *Don Giovanni*.

"risplende ognun sa luce . . ."—"each one gives forth her light which will never die."

Restif—Restif de la Bretonne, the eighteenth-century novelist and libertine, who was called "the Rousseau of the gutter" and "the Voltaire of the chambermaids."

"sola et magna (mater)"—"the one and great mother."

"Gertrude's Mother"—Gertrude Stein and Virgil Thomson did an opera together, *The Mother of Us All*.

"the Virgin & the Whore"—one of Williams's themes in *Paterson*.

"ma basta per oggi . . ."—"enough for today's catalog of girls."

"posh P & O boats"—the Pacific & Orient Line steamers which travelers from England took in the old days. "Posh" stood for "port-side-out-starboard-side-home." Because of the terrible heat in the Red Sea it was desirable to get a cabin on the north side of the ship, away from the sun.

"C'est moi dans la poubelle"—"I'm the one in the trash-can." In the 1960s, after he had become depressed, Pound was in Paris and Beckett took him to a performance of *Endgame*.

"there in the bolge . . ."—Dante tells the story of Bertrand de Born in *Inferno*, XXVIII, 118ff.

"E'l capo tronco . . ."—"Certainly I saw, and to this hour I seem to see, a trunk going headless, even as went the others of that dismal throng, and it held the severed head by the hair, swinging in his hand like a lantern, which looking upon us, said, 'Ah me!' " (Pound's translation, *The Spirit of Romance*, page 45).

"bos chavaliers fo . . ."—"He was a good knight and a good fighter, a good poet and wise and well-spoken." From the *vida* (legendary life) of Bertrand de Born.

San Michele—Pound is buried in the island cemetery of San Michele in the lagoon near Venice.

Dioce—(Deioces in Herodotus) the seventh-century B.C. king of the Medes who revolted against the Assyrians and built the fabulous city of Ecbatana, whose battlements, Herodotus says, "are plated with silver and gold." In Canto LXXIV this becomes: "To build the city of Dioce whose terraces are the colour of stars."

Wagadu—a mythical city in Africa, which Pound learned about from the German anthropologist Leo Frobenius. See Douglas Fox, *African Genesis*.

*"He Did It to Please His Mother"*
Some of the lines are from Shakespeare's *Coriolanus*.

Delmore Schwartz's play was in his first book, *In Dreams Begin Responsibilities* (1938).

Berggasse—Freud lived in the Bergasse in Vienna.

*O Hermes Trismegistus*
Hermes Trismegistus—Hermes, the thrice-greatest, author of the *Hermetic Books* of occult wisdom. Medieval alchemists loved him.

Thoth—the Egyptian god who was possessed of all secret wisdom.

Spatiality, asymptotic, hermeneutic—terms drawn from Structuralism and Semiotics.

# INDEX OF TITLES

246